Barrio Nerds

Barrio Nerds

Latino Males, Schooling, and the Beautiful Struggle

Juan F. Carrillo
School of Education, University of North Carolina, Chapel Hill, USA

SENSE PUBLISHERS
ROTTERDAM/BOSTON/TAIPEI

A C.I.P. record for this book is available from the Library of Congress.

ISBN: 978-94-6300-765-8 (paperback)
ISBN: 978-94-6300-766-5 (hardback)
ISBN: 978-94-6300-767-2 (e-book)

Published by: Sense Publishers,
P.O. Box 21858,
3001 AW Rotterdam,
The Netherlands
https://www.sensepublishers.com/

All chapters in this book have undergone peer review.

Chapter 2 was previously published as: Carrillo, J. F. (2007). Lost in degree: A Chicano Ph.D. student's search for missing clothes. *Journal of Latinos and Education*, *6*(4), 347–350. Reprinted by permission of Taylor & Francis LLC (http://www.tandfonline.com).

Printed on acid-free paper

TABLE OF CONTENTS

ACKNOWLEDGEMENTS

The crafting of words and the thank you have origins in a collaborative-people, spaces, acceptance, rejections, love, and nurture, and that word: pain. This book is a collection of all these things. I write these words as I sit in one important location: Lady Bird Lake (nostalgically and lovingly referred to as "Town Lake"). Draped by the Austin, Texas skyline, turtles in its water, dogs take a swim, people walk, run, and sit on a rock and daydream. It is here where two crucial things happened that made this book possible: I got married (for a second time) and I often found clarity amidst the ambiguity that is writing. There were so many moments when the ideas that are in this book were pushed along as I walked near this waterway, amidst this airwave, amidst the way the sunlight reflected off a creek or over someone's kayak. Water, it has always found its way into my vision. I am blessed that this place found me.

From Town Lake, I begin by thanking my wife. Theorizing, caring, pushing me along, and even draping me with spiritual hope—this book is a manifestation of your love and your immense intelligence. Perhaps this is the world we are given, but when you speak, I am reminded of what initial hope I had for this book: transcendence, healing, naming injustice, and even, clarifying what the song really is so that we could dance, really dance. With this, you helped me write a new chapter-becoming a father again: Natalia and Emiliano, may these words inspire and get you closer and closer to your journey's humanity. I love you all.

In Arizona, I have a group of people that also contributed to this book: my parents, sister, and my sons, Gabriel and Chris. You all have found your way into this book by reminding me of how surreal, glorious, and difficult being alive can be-and you were always there for me as I try to straddle words with the person that I am, the person that I becoming. I love you, may this book help to bridge any distance and incompleteness, and may this book forge new paths for our love. Thank you.

While in graduate school, this book developed its core form as a result of the steadfast mentorship of my committee. Special thanks to Angela Valenzuela, Luis Urrieta, Jr., Cinthia Salinas, Victoria Maria MacDonald, and Iliana Alanís. Your guidance, care, and theoretical support continues to push my ideas along. While not in my formal committee, Douglas Foley also shared jokes, insight, and a constant "Iowa" push – *get it done*, I can hear him say. Thank you.

Richard Rodriguez. You had to write your books for me to write mine. Your prose and vulnerability made more people like me possible. It's crazy. Scholarship boys from California: from one to another, from one generation to another. Where our ideas may differ I still see an audience and that is where the reader decides which lane they will pick and push the stroller down the swirling road. Gracias.

Funding from the Spencer Foundation, various fellowships at the University of Texas at Austin, and an important sabbatical at the University of North Carolina, Chapel Hill made this book possible. I appreciate the support.

Many friends also played an important role in this work. I am particularly indebted to Dave and Rob. You both were willing to take my calls late into the night and provide your feedback. Moreover, the soul of this works in many ways draws from our coming of age and the ways in which we groomed our personalities to be aware, engage art, space, people, human dignity and rights, and feelings with transparency. Also, my friend Macario helped me to see some of the key themes in this book and his brotherly advice make these pages possible in many ways. I will also never forget the comedic part of our friendship – it almost feels like it is a process by which we catch the myths and interrogate our personal growth amidst so many metaphors that constrain the human experience. Gracias.

To working-class Los Angeles, CA – "home." Thank you for the wisdom. To the teachers, the community, the libraries, the swapmeets, it all formed into this and I thank you all for your nurture.

To scholarship boys and girls all over the world: you inspire me. May the words in this book serve as my thank you card.

CHAPTER 1

INTRODUCTION

The Beautiful Struggle

> Haunted by the knowledge that one chooses to become a student. (Education is not an inevitable or natural step in growing up.) Here is a child who cannot forget that his academic success distances him from a life he loved, even from his own memory of himself.
>
> (Rodriguez, 1982, p. 48)

TOLL FEES AND INTERSECTING ROADS

My words have motion because I saw jellyfish at a young age. These moving things that sting have always drawn my attention. Water, flow, swimming through "pipelines" and schooling trajectories of gain and loss. This is a love letter. This is a collection of stories. I have collected dead ends and roads with toll fees. I also made it to a little Mexican coastal town as morning drank coffee; I still spiritually connect with the waves, the Spanish that bounced around the air. The blue in the sky. The crude softness of time. I am writing this book for the existential searchers. I deliver a message across borders and living rooms. I am in Taos, New Mexico, I am in Los Angeles, California, I am in São Paulo, Brazil, I am in Ciudad Juárez, Mexico: in prisons, in schools, in countries where a "slum," a barrio, a ghetto, is *home*. This book is about a universal language around hope and sadness, triumph and ambivalence. These words are for the poets, the kids with skittles in their side pocket, the skaters, and all those watching the movie with a wideshot. There are also the "professionals" caught navigating myths of success – some of you have dark secrets. At 1 am you walk through an alley in your soul; you wander in an out of your own innocence, those intimate moments of childhood in working-class contexts narrate your ongoing questions of who you are, where you are, how you talk, how you feel and think. You may feel alone and homeless. These voices. These feelings have expiration and rebirth dates. Mother: where are you? This city of lost of angels has killed many. This book is a telling and coming to terms, or maybe just a way to meet new friends.

Today, I am a father, son, husband, and I have a professional title of "academic." But I hope you feel so free in the way I water the literary lawn. I purposely will try to evade dry academic prose in some of these pages. I channel the floor. I recently saw my father on the floor after he drank too much. This was the day before Christmas. It was just us two. I felt a certain sadness – the quiet of holiday season is terrifying amidst all the mall congestion. He yelled at monsters that were near him. He asked me for money, not for my resume. He does not understand what I do. He did not attend my PhD graduation. He will likely never read this book. My mother tells me about her hometown in rural Sinaloa, Mexico – she dreams of living there full-time. She just moved to the United States for some health insurance, not for an "American Dream." Or maybe, I should not speak for her. I write journal articles and she tells me that the birds, the sounds of the birds, she asks that I please listen to that and send her money as well. In this house there was never any wine, just beer bottles with trails into dark deliverance. It's beautiful, it's painful, I miss it, it is hollow and rich. I sleep in a cold room with sheets full of tiger images.

These words are bred in travels. In Mexico there is always a place for me to eat menudo. These spaces with open windows and the Mexican soul have a redemptive spiritual prose: I come back to its unpredictability as a U.S. born son. Some of this writing came from Mexico. I sat there, in Ciudad Juárez, in Guadalajara, nurtured by my fear and confidence in opening more of the envelope of "success" that came to this barrio boy from L.A. My mother tells me that I was a good kid. I was born in a county hospital. I see the food stamps, I see my father in jail for drinking and driving, it caught up to him. I hear screams. I hear about no money to pay the bills. I take long walks as an eight year old hoping to find love, home, and safety. Thank God for that southern California weather – that sun and breeze always left an imprint in my soul. As I move and move, I still claim California. These words now come to mind:

> There is no water left in the high song of little birds carrying water for the children of men and boys in Havana. After all that running the river had an ocean to take on a date. All these beautiful stars have memory. Melancholic hair stains on the side of palm trees at midnight. Even this powder becomes presence. Off your side we can. We gain already, momentum…

What more am I suppose to say in this introduction? I do not like umbrellas. And like Samuel Beckett, I do run with words and existentialism at various points. I am not in a rush, but yet I kind of am. My three year-old son Emiliano tells me that on a Monday, and only on a Monday that never comes, that he will attend school. As I write about Latino males in U.S.

schools, as I put words to the page, I want less detachment, more emotion, more physical access to discomfort and vulnerability. These words are my own. I claim every single word. Moreover, I have never liked action movies but I like acting. I am confused about the process and where the actual "being" takes place. I bare witness as I see a Latino male in his 40's sitting on a chair at a Barnes and Noble bookstore in Raleigh, North Carolina. He reads through a comic book and after an hour, he walks to the food court where he will serve chow mein to seniors that fast-walk across the mall to keep their blood pressure in tact. I am around all these *things* as state legislators continue to defund public education and the BMW 3 series has an increase in sales.

In this book, I have four primary objectives: (1) centering an additive framework, (2) moving beyond clean-victory narratives, (3) identifying systemic challenges and opportunities, and (4) creating opportunities for dialogue related to developing spaces and policies that nurture holistic success narratives and manhood development among/with Latino males. As such, I am interested in going beyond retention and good-will narratives of access within the system as it is, but I instead question the costs, recognize the gains, and complicate the terror and opportunities that lie in formal education and social-class mobility via schooling for Latino male youth. Moreover, I position community, roots, and identity at the center of ambition and academic excellence. I am ok with contradictions and clean stage theories are not part of this book. Additionally, I agree with Gladwell (2013) that "…being an underdog can *change* people in ways that we often fail to appreciate: it can open doors and create opportunities and educate and enlighten and make possible what might otherwise have seemed unthinkable" (p. 6). This philosophy is important for it moves away from deficit ideas around low-income students of color, but nonetheless, we must also stress the importance of holding social structures and institutions accountable.

Emailing and Meeting Richard Rodriguez

My interest in conducting research on Latino males started from examining my own trajectory. I am the first person in my immediate family to graduate from third grade. My memories are those that take me to swapmeets where we sold shoes, security guard pat-downs as I entered my high school campus, and lots of melancholia around my realization that Mexicans were a disliked group. Things were heavy from the start and I had to make sense of it or die trying. I grew up on welfare in the barrios of South Los Angeles, California and I attended public schools in low-income communities. I loved to read and write at a young age and most of my friends were not college bound. Today, some of my childhood friends are mariachi singers, factory workers, and one that I will affectionately call "little red" disappeared into the prison system. This book is the culmination of my own anxieties, frustrations, and inner and "outer" work. I channel my friendships, the love they give me, and the struggle and pain that they still inform me with.

Moreover, this this book also has roots within the work of Richard Rodriguez. In 2004, I was coming off a divorce. I packed my Honda Accord and left Phoenix, Arizona for Tallahassee, Florida. My friend David and Robert came along. We stopped in New Orleans, took a break in San Antonio. I almost fainted in S.A. from the fatigue and emotionally taxing process that I was engaging in. I was going to graduate school as I was kind of losing everything – my "home," my spouse, and my two sons. Still, our destination was Tallahassee, Florida. I was offered admission into Florida State University's Educational Leadership and Policy Studies doctoral program. I spent one year there. And during this year, my girlfriend at the time encouraged me to me to write an email to Richard Rodriguez. Dazed by time and the melancholic airs of what it means to move away from my family, nostalgia and reflection began to set in. I grabbed an old copy of Rodriguez's (1982) *Hunger of Memory* from the trunk of my car and I re-read the section, *Achievement of Desire*. It changed me forever. I wrote Rodriguez a letter via e-mail. I wanted to reclaim some of my past and begin to unpack my "scholarship boy" journey.

After making this strong reflective connection evident to Richard Rodriguez, he replied via e-mail to introduce our intellectual relationship:

> My dear Juan, through the gray ether of cyberspace I am happy to meet you. Your amiga, Erica, was right. We are shadows, the one of the other, separated by seasons – coming or going. (I am January; you are May). Though I flatter myself to dare the comparison. You seem capable of a humor and ease and charm that I could never manage. (I cannot imagine writing an email to my own Richard Rodriguez – James Baldwin – when I was in graduate school and 28 years old.) I was a dull young man, indeed, afraid to discover my voice or even my body. I was never naked, intellectually or to the brown sun overhead. And your father trumps mine by a year! Mine had two years of grammar school in Mexico. Damn Mexico! Mistreating so much talent and youth. But the reason I wrote HUNGER OF MEMORY is that I could not find it on the library shelf, when I needed, in my thirties, to find it. So I wrote the book that I yearned to read. Thank you for now reading my life,

> despite the protestations of your dreadful professor. (You should sue such teachers and demand your tuition money back.) I don't know that I like Richard Rodriguez. I don't even think he is such a likable fellow. But he spoke the truth in HUNGER OF MEMORY, despite the chorus of the politically correct who would deny him. I am in awe today of his ability to tell the truth. You. I am proud that you are my reader. I am even more pleased that you managed to find your way out of the labyrinth of Compton. I notice that your affection for Los Angeles is nonetheless undiminished. I imagine you in your Lakers jersey. My basketball team, alas, does not exist. D.H. Lawrence at center. Octavio Paz. Jimmy Baldwin. Joan Didion. W.M. Thackeray. I would happily be water boy for such players. You are right about long letters or email. They swallow the air. So I will be quiet. Someday I hope to meet up with you. I don't get to Tallahassee Though Miami, yes. More likely, perhaps, we can meet up when you are in L.A. on a visit to your familia. I wish you more bravery than I could manage at 28, and continued success, in the meanwhile. Your life is chapter two of the story. Tell me someday. Richard (personal communication, 2004).

And with that, I ended up transferring to the University of Texas at Austin a year later and working my way towards a dissertation that focuses on scholarship boys. Moreover, while I was beginning my career as an assistant professor at the University of North Carolina Chapel Hill, I got to meet Richard Rodriguez in San Francisco, CA. I was nervous on that spring day. I was going to meet the author, the controversial figure, Richard Rodriguez. We had dinner at a Thai place near his home. He was generous, charismatic, and projected a cosmopolitan air not too different from his prose. On that day, I reflected on the encounter in this manner:

> All boys need access to a writer who they eventually get to meet. Then, the writer walks away on Bush Street. Wearing jeans, a glare towards the ground, and his prose lies fixed on a rubber band that still withers through my doors of perception. There is a vacant bench in San Francisco. I sit and look left. Well, "good-bye." The hills take him to the pastoral syllable yet to come. I stare at my hands and the cracks on the paved road. It's a wrinkle-in-time, a freckle stamped on the fleeting, "why me and what now?"

I have known Richard Rodriguez for many years now. My scholarship boy journey continues and this work is a reflection of the reading, writing, and my somewhat surreal link with Richard Rodriguez.

CONTRIBUTIONS OF PRIOR SCHOLARSHIP

Learning about the Lives of Latino Males

President Barack Obama's *My Brother's Keeper Initiative* is a reminder of the stressors, systemic threats, and opportunities for collaborative efforts in positively impacting the lives of males of color. Additionally, as Sáenz and Ponjuan (2011) point out, boys, generally, are "…twice as likely as girls to be labeled 'learning disabled,' they are seven times more likely to be diagnosed with attention deficit disorder or attention hyperactive disorder, they constitute up to 67 percent the special education population, and in school systems they are up to 10 times more likely to be diagnosed with serious emotional and behavioral disorders" (p. 7). Over the last few years, there has been a growth in the work that specifically addresses the experiences of Latino males in U.S. schools (Carrillo, 2010, 2013; Conchas & Vigil, 2012; Rios, 2011; Sáenz & Ponjuán, 2008; Noguera, Hurtado, & Fergus, 2012; Rios, 2011; Ríos Vega, 2015; Sáenz, Ponjuán, & Figueroa, 2016; Peréz II, 2014). This work has provided important contributions related to the importance of different forms of social capital, additive frameworks, mentoring, community cultural wealth, peer-support and friendships. This is a pivotal area of inquiry in light of the fact that in U.S. K-12 public schools, non-Whites are now the majority of students and Latin@s make up the majority of the student body in public schools in states like California and have significantly changed the demographics of schools across the rural south (http://www.sfgate.com/education/article/Latino-kids-now-majority-in-state-s-public-schools-3166843.php; http://www.edweek.org/ew/articles/2014/08/20/01demographics.h34.html; http://ui.uncc.edu/story/hispanic-latino-population-north-carolina-cities-census).

The Case of the Scholarship Boy

Much of this book is also informed by scholarship boy work. Hoggart (1957/2006) coined the term in his essay, "The Uprooted and Anxious," describing scholarship boys as acutely conscious of how school has changed them. He focused on 20th century British students who start off as working-class sons of warm and rich environments only to be removed from much of this context by their interactions and mobility through the schooling structure. Based on Hoggart's analysis, they usually excel in different ways, and at different points, in the school setting. School becomes a big part of their identity. The schooling experience posits scholarship boys at the "friction point of two cultures" (Hoggart, 1957/2006, p. 225). That is, they are caught between cultural and social class contact zones that often evoke feelings of intense dislocation. Unlike most social scientists which have a particular research site from which to interpret and to draw implications, Hoggart does not study a specific locale with explicit mention of field notes or other technical documentation. Instead, he takes a general interpretation of a phenomenon which appears to be largely based on intuition, informed by his own scholarship boy journey from the British working-class to the professoriate. Moreover, Hoggart, a giant in the realm of cultural studies (some believe he coined the very term, "cultural studies"), adopts a literary approach.

Relying on Hoggart, Rodriguez (1982) first applied the "scholarship-boy" term to Latin@s. His essay, *Going Home Again: The New American Scholarship Boy* (1975) served as the catalyst for his seminal work, *Hunger of Memory* (1982), where he painfully explored the psychic, cultural, and the emotional costs he paid for separation from his working-class family while pursuing "excellence" in school. For Rodriguez, it was his contact with Hoggart's (1957/2006) scholarship boy concept that set him on a truly unique path. The nostalgia of his childhood and the disconnect he felt in the sterile, European libraries where he tried to pen his dissertation, resulted in him leaving his Ph.D. program. Longing for the hues, the rhythms, and the sentiment of his working-class origins, he developed an existential angst and sought refuge by becoming an isolated writer, poised to make his individualistic mark on the discourse revolving the experiences of academically successful Mexican American students. Indeed, his life is the embodiment of how social class and education lead to the modification of language, class standing, and consciousness. Rodriguez reacted to a time in which the Third World studies movement was taking shape at Berkeley. His coping strategy was partly based in the dichotomous way in which he argued that there should be a separation between the private and public self. He argued that language and cultural ties should be fostered in the private arena, while the public face should require an Americanization process that leads to the promised land: "success." Rodriguez's own contradictory statements in other works position this comment as somewhat of a period piece, vested in a time in which he felt alone and angry at the violent way in which schooling had removed him from his past. Working off this anger, it could be argued that Rodriguez collapsed, leading to a painful and public exposé of his injuries.

Rodriguez's cathartic manifesto, *Hunger of Memory* (1982), exposed "secrets," contradictions, and an incoherence that does not fit neatly into the fundamentalist sector of Chicana/o nationalist ideology, simplistic models of social class mobility, or romanticized arguments on assimilation. Rodriguez's conservative stances on Affirmative Action and Bilingual Education are major reasons why exploration of the scholarship boy experience has been left largely unexplored by researchers. Critics have also obsessed with his views on identity politics without taking a nuanced approach to how Rodriguez was unable to fully assimilate into U.S. society. Even though Rodriguez contends that the private self needs to be lost for the sake of the promise of a successful public identity, his painful scholarship boy journey suggests that he was passionate about recovering his cultural connections to his working class, Mexican-origin past and he never fully become part of the mythical and problematic, melting pot. In fact, most of his books and articles deal with Latin@ issues. He is writing from the "outside" about a group (Mexican-origin people) that are still "outside" of the power structure of the dominant class. In many ways, he is caught in a contradictory self-dialogue. Nonetheless, it is clear that Rodriguez does want to "mainstream" his identity and not be attached to "disadvantaged" and "outsider" labels. This book, on the other hand, examines the lives of Mexican-origin scholarship boys that consciously attempt to reconcile the intersections of race and ethnicity, class, and gender, seeking a less static and subtractive way by which to become an "educated" person in the United States.

Scholarship boy research has also been expanded to include work on Latina scholarship girls (Cuádraz & Pierce, 1994; Cuádraz, 1996, 1999, 2006; Rendón, 1992). These studies have applied the scholarship boy concept to the experiences of university-trained women of working-class origin. Cuádraz's (1993) case study research on Chicana/o scholarship boys and girls that entered doctoral programs at the University of California at Berkeley between 1967 and 1979 demonstrated the alienating nature of graduate school for many students. Three quarters of the students came from working-class backgrounds and the majority maintained a life-long Chicana/o based identity (p. 264). Nonetheless, for those that became academics, they struggled with the dislocation of being framed as "outsiders" to the knowledge factory. While Rodriguez found assimilation to be a worthy reward, the sample in Cuádraz's study consisted of a politicized Chicana/o professoriate and professional class that fought for a more pluralistic identity alongside social change informed largely by the Chicana/o movement. Cuádraz's sample maintained a consistency in their politicized consciousness as opposed to Rodriguez who became disillusioned.

Cuádraz's (1993) important work drew on the politics of the time in which the "affirmative action babies" that made up her sample entered a university space that had historically closed the doors to Latinos. Her work demonstrates how students pained at the feelings related to tokenism, gender, racial, political, and class dislocation as the institution failed to be sensitive to their needs. What is interesting and relevant to this research is how some scholarship boys appear to not sense an intellectual inferiority or unpreparedness compared to their white peers (as many do in Cuádraz's study). Instead, many of them feel a sense of "smartness" beyond the middle-class ontology germane to the Euro-American journey which they feel appropriates them (Mexican-origin scholarship boys) at an elevated level of consciousness and intelligence. Along the same lines, scholarship boys, such as Rodriguez (1982) and Carrillo (2007) allude to some of this.

Rendón (1992) also applied the scholarship boy concept to her own scholarship girl experiences. She questioned the static assimilation notions that she believes Rodriguez supports. She contends that the adaptation process should not force only Latino students to adapt, but the university should also address some of the cultural tensions that scholarship boys and girls face. Like other scholarship boys and girls, she experienced years of isolation, loneliness, and humiliation. She agrees with Rodriguez in that scholarship boys and girls are often left with only the nostalgic "hunger of memory," which entails a longing for the closeness and intimacy of one's parents and "former" life. She contends that she does not fit into this group, for she carries her past with her everywhere she goes. While Rendón (1992) says that she looks to the future instead of the past, it appears that scholarship boys who are still graduate students find it much harder than some faculty to simply say, "I do not yearn for the past." While nostalgia is not a trait of the exclusive domain of scholarship boys, what remains quite salient is the way reminiscing on the past stirs their conscientization process related to the culturally subtractive experiences that they appear to associate with schooling and from aspiring to becoming "highly educated" (for examples, see Rodriguez, 1975, 1982; Hoggart, 1957; Carrillo, 2007).

It is quite clear that the university space illuminates troubling personal feelings for scholarship boys. According to Feagin, Vera and Imani (1996), "the physical and social spaces of predominantly white colleges and universities generally embody the presumption of one-way assimilation for students of color" (p. 51). Along these lines, Reyes III (2013) explored how a scholarship boy, Ruben, who is part of College Assistance Migrant Program (CAMP) encounters many tensions related to "making it" within a Whitestream university setting. For Ruben, there is confluence and clash of values between home and school life. These tensions are embodied and often elicit intense emotional, spiritual, cultural, and psychic costs. This book will in part counter the discourses that claim that this type of assimilation is a healthy mechanism by which students of color will achieve "success" in U.S. public life and schools. Hence, for the purpose of this book, assimilation will be analyzed in the dialectical sense, as a process that is continuously being processed, contested, and negotiated.

From Rodriguez and Hoggart, we can gather that a central problem that scholarship boys face is the straddling of the working-class culture of their origin with the middle-class space of academia. What initially seems like an innocent "move up" transforms into an arduous personal assessment of how much a scholarship boy has been removed from their past. Hoggart melded his own experiences together with his cultural intuition to develop the scholarship boy concept, but does not use empirical data or triangulation methods to examine the scholarship boy phenomenon. Rodriguez provides a compelling treatise, but it is the voice of one man and his memories, reflecting both its strengths and its limitations. Mexican-origin scholarship boys, as exemplified by Rodriguez, live out a complex web of contradictions in conjunction with navigating a plethora of philosophical negotiations and identities throughout their educational life course.

Social Reproduction

Social reproduction theorists address academic underachievement by drawing on how the class structure is reproduced from generation to generation through socializing nature of hidden and overt curriculum in schools. This school of thought draws heavily from Marx, Weber, and Durkheim. Theorists (Apple, 1978; Bernstein, 1975; Bowles & Gintis, 1976; Bourdieu, 1977; Macleoud, 1995; Anyon, 1997; Oakes, 2005) that are part of this school of thought demonstrate how some groups benefit and some do not due to schooling structures/mechanisms that reproduce the social structure. The school site is considered to be a primary site of social class reproduction and low academic performance. The political economic theorists, Bowles and Gintis, argue in Schooling in Capitalist America (1976) that lower class students are socialized in schooling structures to meet the needs of a lower class labor market. Similarly, the curriculum theorist Michael Apple (1978), contends that high status knowledge is distributed unequally, helping to reproduce a socially stratified society. While this may be true in some respects, it appears that scholarship boys do not "automatically" mimic lower or working-class social trajectories. Though a working-class past informs their journeys, they embody a more eclectic interaction with socializing sites such as schools. Many attended low SES urban schools, but did not end up becoming part of the low-income workforce. Hence, it is appropriate to argue that much of this work is deterministic and bounded through its substantial economic focus and an insufficient focus on the role of human agency. Notable critiques have come from scholars like Willis (1977) who conceptualized more flexible approaches to reproduction theory by suggesting that working-class students exercise their agency through schooling orientations that mediate their academic outcomes. Willis argues that they create and participate as subjects when making many of their choices.

In addition, parental input offers potential influence on school site reproduction. Gibson's (1988) ethnographic study of Punjabi immigrants in a California high school demonstrates the orchestration of the concept known as "accommodation without assimilation." The parents of Punjabi students encouraged academic success all while also expecting their children to maintain their cultural ways and connections to their community (Gibson, 1988). While the economic reproduction theory underscores the importance of tracking mechanisms, a factor that is salient in my scholarship boy work that is particularly useful is research like Willis's (1977) and Gibson's (1988) that accords emphasis to students' and parents' responses as mediating factors in educational outcomes. These studies unpack the conceptual space for the kind of agency that I investigate herein in my analysis of the trajectories of scholarship boys.

Notwithstanding the determinism within cultural reproduction theory, Bourdieu's concept of cultural capital is also relevant to this research study. Specifically, Bourdieu (1984), a cultural theorist, defines cultural capital as a set of dispositions congruent with a person's social class. The "recognition" of certain types of cultural capital translates into a higher likelihood of attaining academic success. Familiarity with and incorporation into a dominant class notion of cultural capital provide the highest prospects for doing well in school. There is reason to believe that contrary to Bourdieu's (1984) argument that the working classes are bounded by the extraordinary realism of their enclosed opportunity field, Mexican-origin scholarship boys embody a multiplicity and elastic dialogic with their social class and life chances. There appears to not be the static identity tropes that Bourdieu associates with working-class individuals.

Scholarship boys in this proposed study come from working-class backgrounds and their parents have low levels of formal schooling. Based on this social reproduction lens, they would tend to be at a "disadvantage" in school settings. Anyon's (1997) ethnographic work on "ghetto schooling" shows that the low status cultural capital of inner-city youth is in part transmitted through schools that socialize students into working-class jobs through limits placed on their academic experiences. Oakes' (2005) ethnographic study on academic tracking in twenty five schools (middle schools and high schools) also concludes that racial minorities are over represented in low academic tracks where they receive an inferior education, ultimately affecting their leveled aspirations. What is interesting about scholarship boys, is that unlike the lads in Willis' research (1977) or the vatos in Foley's (1990) study of a South Texas high school, scholarship boys appear to resist bounded and linear notions of assimilation all while not rejecting in absolute terms, the schooling process. Their resistance does not come at the expense of failing classes or dropping out of high school (or college). They do not fit neatly into the cultural reproduction theories mentioned here.

Along these lines, contrary to what Bourdieu would predict, the scholarship boys in my study did attend "ghetto schools" but proved able to attain high levels of educational achievement. It may have been their cultural capital and its connection to a certain type of habitus (Bourdieu, 1984) or other factors like their passionate contestation of assimilation into the dominant class's social mores may have come into play. Although informative, Bourdieu's cultural capital lacks the complexity to accurately account for the ways that scholarship boys may in fact possess an elastic construction of cultural capital that is well-suited within their contexts.

Based on Hoggart's (1957/2006) work, we gather that they embody more than "one type" of cultural capital and do not merely wait for "transmission" stages, as posited by Bourdieu. Their hybrid identities appear to disrupt the static correlations that Bourdieu makes. Instead, a "role-playing cleverness" or a "double consciousness" or multiple consciousness may account for a certain type of giftedness not captured by traditional measurements. That is, these students appear to develop a strong grasp of the cultural capital of various social groups, leading to distinct dispositions and behaviors in school, home, and among peer groups with "successful" results. Following this line of thought, habiti formation is eclectic and less restrained by the dogmatic, structuralist notions that Bourdieu's otherwise important work explores.

CULTURAL-ECOLOGICAL PERSPECTIVE

This theoretical lens is primarily situated within work of the late John Ogbu (1978, 1987). From this school of thought, the argument is that "... differences in academic achievement result from minority group's initial incorporation into U.S. society and minority group's perceptions of the limited opportunity structure" (Conchas, 2006, p. 10). Ogbu (1987) distinguishes between voluntary immigrants, such as Japanese, Koreans, and Chinese, and involuntary immigrants, like African Americans, Chicanos, and Native Americans. While voluntary immigrants came to the U.S. by choice and develop optimism toward U.S. institutions, involuntary immigrants came to the U.S. via slavery, colonialism, and conquest, thus forging a resistance to assimilation that presumably explains, in part, their disdain for school. Both their historic and their present relationship with U.S. society suggests to them that they have limited opportunities compared to white peers, thereby severing the link between their predictably high aspirations and their levels of effort directed toward achieving those aspirations.

In Ogbu's view (1987, 1991), these macro psychosocial processes explain the low academic achievement of involuntary minorities and as a consequence, the caste-like status of their communities. Fordham and Ogbu's (1986) ethnographic study of African American youth in a Washington D.C. high school also illuminates some of these dimensions by examining the burden of "acting white" which often leads to diminishing effort translating into academic underachievement. While Ogbu's theorizing has been critiqued for being very deterministic (Foley, 1991; Trueba, 1988), his notions of oppositionality and adaptational coping mechanisms have currency in this study of scholarship boys. Working off of Ogbu's work, it important to point out that some Mexican-origin scholarship boys appear to also experience the burden of "acting white," while not outright rejecting their role as "successful" students. Some Mexican-origin scholarship boys appear to use education (through formal schooling) as a means by which to unpack the burden of being forced to "act white."

LATIN@ EDUCATION SCHOLARSHIP

Latina/o scholars also have made significant contributions to understanding Latin@ student achievement (Solórzano, 1992; Moll, Amanti, Neff, & Gonzalez, 1992; Gándara, 1995; Valenzuela, 1999; Stanton-Salazar, 2001; Villenas, 2001; Yosso, 2006; Conchas, 2006). While much of this research explores issues of caring, identity, parental support, cultural relevance, and network strategies, an abiding concern that runs through this scholarship is with the coercive demand that youth assimilate implicitly, and oftentimes explicitly, to a curriculum structured to induce cultural de-identification (Valenzuela, 1999) or cultural erasure (Bartolomé, 1998). Given that culture and class overlap closely in the case of Latina/os, and children of color, generally, this expectation is tantamount to class erasure as well. Hoggart conveys this deep angst about class erasure while Rodriguez' conundrum is additionally characterized by issues of language and of cultural identity. Additionally, Valencia's (1997) seminal work on deficit thinking illuminates the ideological deficits that teachers may have towards their Latino students. Although insightful regarding the dynamics that enter into the impact of schooling on identity negotiations that youth must undertake, this scholarship does not address scholarship boy research. This books fills in this gap and also in part, explores the under-examined context of the successes and pain of the "winners." In spite of all the subtractive forces mentioned in this foundational area of inquiry, Mexican-origin scholarship boys do "make it." That is, they achieve academic excellence as measured by their attainment of graduate levels of education in spite systemic obstacles. In some ways, their journeys coincide somewhat with Yosso's (2005) additive concept of *community cultural wealth* which demonstrates how many working-class, students of color do not lack the necessary cultural capital to engage in social class mobility but instead, they draw from multiple forms of capital (aspirational, familial, social, linguistic, resistant, and navigational) that provide pivotal guidance in achieving their goals.

GIFTED LATIN@ LITERATURE

The controversial area of giftedness will be covered in this book. To this end, this section examines literature written on gifted Latin@ students because it provides a tremendous resource for examining the scholarship boy's experience. I consider difficulties and biases in the psychological measurement of giftedness, as well as conceptual developments in this area, including the work of scholar Gardner (1985), whose theorizing has expanded on deterministic notions of intelligence. I also examine the limitations innate to Gardner's attempt to "objectively" hone in on "intelligence." Giftedness is in and of itself a problematic concept, laced with imperialistic and colonial dimensions that have violently disposed many students of color from the quality education they deserve. It is important to analyze how and why prevailing notions of giftedness continue to benefit particular groups of students based on race and class and other intersecting categories. I unpack the Western model of giftedness, which often fails to account for human diversity and complexity. These measures may be just assessing a certain ontology and/or cultural capital and attributing a misguided giftedness label. Moreover, Hatt (2011) reminds us that "smartness" or ideas around intelligence are cultural productions, which often are layered with unequal power relations that frame self-identity and social positioning.

According to Valencia, Villarreal and Salinas (2002), "since the 1920's, the amount of research concerning the general field of giftedness has been, and continues to be, relatively small compared to the total number of citations in the psychological and educational literature. This research base, however, shrinks significantly when delimited to those citations that include racial/ethnic minority students" (p. 281). This research gap continues today leading to grand generalizations. Among the most controversial contemporary scholars are Jensen (1998) and Herrnstein and Murray (1994), who explicitly overstate the implications of the I.Q. measure. Their argument germane to "white" superiority in intelligence places them within an intellectual blind spot. Their line of thought on intelligence is dogmatic and laced with a serious lack of reflexivity and complexity. Clearly, their assessments are tainted with the ontological limitations of history, race, class, and gender. The cultural production of intelligence continues to leave out the culturally situated "intelligences" of students of color. Thus, this paucity in scholarship mirrors Latinos' low levels of representation among all students identified as gifted. When only 8.56 percent of all students classified as gifted are Latinos (U.S. Department of Education, 1999), the shocking racial disparity between identified Anglo and Latin@ gifted students constitutes a serious concern. Moreover, when Latin@ students are placed in gifted programming, they often have to deal with various microagressions related to ethnicity and intelligence (Carrillo & Rodriguez, 2016).

Most school districts use standardized tests and IQ scores to measure giftedness (Staiger, 2004). Deterministic definitions of giftedness have resulted in the production of "...'false negatives:' children who, indeed are gifted but whose potentials go unrecognized and uncultivated by the schools" (Bernal, 1980, p. 6). Some of the research suggests that degree of acculturation by students (Bernal & Reyna, 1976; Mercer, 1976), teacher perceptions of giftedness (Brigss & Reiss, 2004; Ford, 1994), and the operationalization of "whiteness" as giftedness (Staiger, 2004), discriminates against students of color, all of which considerably compound the very problem. As dominant notions of giftedness track certain students into "success" tracks, many students of color are provided consequently receive an inferior education.

Valencia (2002) also discusses the role that parents play in nominating students for gifted programs. Latino parents are less likely (as compared to white parents) to nominate their children for gifted programs. Much of this stems from a lack of information to guide them to action on their children's behalf. Moreover, Bernal (1979) maintains that there is a "cognitive dissonance" related to many educators' beliefs that there are no gifted students of color. By this, he means that giftedness does not equate to students of color. Valencia (2002) urges a "principle of affirmation" to retard this deficit construct. By this he means that all students are gifted until deemed otherwise. Possessing a deficit orientation adversely affects the potential of recognizing gifted Latino students. Broadened, research-based conceptualizations of giftedness could better account for the talents that scholarship boys possess and result in appropriate educational services on par with mainstream gifted students. As Kaplan (1974) suggests, gifted and talented students need to be measured in the "...context of their own culture..." (p. 79). For the Mexican-origin scholarship boy, the inroads of race and class mediate his distinctive cultural context. Hence, there is a need for constructing instruments that are culturally sensitive in terms of administration and measurement (Padilla, 2001).

The Latino gifted literature helps to point out the limitations in one of the most popular frameworks related to assessing intelligence, Gardner's central work, Frames of Mind (1985). In this work, Gardner lays out his multiple intelligences framework. His postdoctoral work led him to acquire a keen interest in neurology and in the biological and psychological dimensions of ability. While his foregrounding of his work in these areas is important, the sociocultural dimensions of his model are under-examined. Along these lines, what Hoggart and Rodriguez suggest about scholarship boys is an intense and critical understanding of the process by which social rituals influence their identity. The MI model does not properly assess a scholarship boy who may possess a more critical set of intelligences that are not marked by static categories, but instead, hybrid interactions with multiple culture worlds, contradictions, and different forms of knowledge. Moreover, Gardner's provocative work does not culturally situate intelligence for he takes an objectivist approach. As such, he assumes that his intelligences are "neutral" and "value-free" expressions that come from simply being highly talented.

Gardner's multiple intelligences (MI) framework consists of eight different kinds of intelligence that he has identified in his own research as follows: bodily-kinesthetic, interpersonal, linguistic, logical-mathematical, naturalistic, intrapersonal, spatial, and musical. Gardner did attempt to examine other intelligences like morality and existentialism, but he had difficulties with the codification of these dimensions. Gardner credits his fascination with the arts for inspiring him to explore a multidimensional model of intelligence. Clearly, his work derives its strengths and serious limitations by its bounded association with developmental psychology.

Drawing from Rodriguez and Hoggart, there is reason to believe that scholarship boys may have exceptional abilities in the areas of: critical consciousness, sociological intuition, and ethics. Scholarship boys seem to be able to deconstruct the world and its impact on individuals with passionate and sensitive clarity. It is this critical consciousness and sociological intuition that forges some of them to have an ethical, strong-willed perception of what role assimilation should have in their lives. Whereas Rodriguez refused to let activists assimilate him into their version of Latinidad, Hoggart wrestled with the ways in which he can come to terms with a double consciousness that makes sense to him.

LIMITATIONS OF PRIOR SCHOLARSHIP

It is important to note that neither the social-reproduction nor cultural-ecological perspectives seem to adequately examine the fundamental issues germane to the scholarship boy experience: multiple consciousness, the costs and gains of academic success, and tensions embedded in social class mobility. While research on scholarship girls bears some relevance, Rendón (1992) provides solely a first-hand account of her experiences and Cuádraz (1996) does not unpack notions of giftedness related to scholarship boys and girls. What they do very well, nonetheless, is exposing the multiple marginalities that scholarship boys and girls experience. Though different terms are deployed, parallel constructions related to personal alienation—as conveyed by Sennet and Cobb's (1972) notion of "hidden injuries of class"—pervade much of this line of research. For Mexican-origin scholarship boys, the "class injuries" intersect with race and ethnicity and masculinities. Additionally, I stress again that there is rarely a connection made between giftedness and academic success for these socially mobile students. Hence, this book will in part, demonstrate how Mexican-origin scholarship boys merge street smarts and schools smarts in ways that are pivotal for academic success. This process is a battle over the self, a love for community knowledge and history, the ambivalent and painful process of staying "true" to the past even as it merges with the present, and the power to name and claim roots in ways that are enriching, lucid, and not so subtractive.

Methods and Scholarship Boy Portraits

Chapters 3–5 draw from semi-structured life history (Hatch & Wisnieski, 2002) interviews of Mexican-origin scholarship boys that earned a graduate level education. Interviews were conducted from March 2008 to March 2009. Two of the scholarship boys are professors that earned a PhD, one has a master's degree in Media Arts, and the other graduate student is currently working on his PhD in Curriculum and Instruction at a top-tier university in the U.S. Southwest. I use pseudonyms throughout this book to protect the privacy of the participants. All of the scholarship boys grew up in working-class communities and attended K-12 public schools in urban, low SES communities. Also, I used a convenience sample and a *snowball sampling* (Weiss, 1994) process. For more detailed information on the methods process, please see Carrillo (2010).

Brief Scholarship Boy Portraits

In Chapters 3, 4, and 5, I will draw from scholarship boy interview data. Note that in Chapter 5, only David, Carlos, and Mario are covered. Below, I provide brief portraits of each scholarship boy.

Mario is a middle school principal. His father gave him a middle name in honor of a Latin American revolutionary. Mario has long been active in statewide politics and activism within schools and in the larger community. He was a former teacher of the year at an elementary school located in his home community. He was born and raised in a major, urban, southwestern U.S. city. He still lives there today and is currently working on a PhD in curriculum and instruction at a nearby university. Cesar Chavez and Saul Alinksy are some of his biggest inspirations.

David is a professor emeritus at a top-tier university located in the southwestern United States. He is one of the pioneers of Chicano Studies and was active in the Chicano movement. He earned a PhD in Political Science from what he refers to as a "conservative" program located within a prestigious university on the west coast of the U.S.

Carlos is an associate professor of human development at a university located in the southwestern U.S. He earned a PhD in Education from a top-tier university located on the west coast of the U.S. He is a first-generation college graduate. Like all the Latino males in this sample, he grew up in low-income communities and he attended public schools (K-12). His research, activism, and teaching is embedded within social justice principles, with a significant passion and commitment to the Latin@ community.

Antonio grew up in two major urban areas in the U.S. southwest. He is a charismatic, sarcastic, and a fast talking scholarship boy who merges street knowledge with more mainstream, university content in very engaging ways. His journey into earning a master's degree in Media Arts from a research-intensive university is somewhat improbable considering that he spent many years in K-12 schools labeled as a "special education" student and was often tracked into vocational classes. He remembers very few advocates within his K-12 schooling experience but instead often reminded me that the local public library and his room were his spaces of liberation, knowledge, and the creative engines for developing his emancipatory dreamworlds. Antonio currently works as an independent filmmaker.

What brings all these scholarship boys together is how they merge their stories, their struggles, their ambivalence, intelligences, and their pain in ways that lead to humanization and ongoing struggle for social justice. In the ensuing section, I provide more details about what I will cover in each chapter of this book.

Book Outline

Chapter 1, "Introduction: The Beautiful Struggle," encompasses this chapter that you are currently reading through. I hope that this section provides some clarity around how my work is situated in a larger body of work, how it extends it in some areas, and also provides a glimpse to what is yet to come.

Chapter 2, "Lost in Degree," sets us up for what comes later. This essay explores my own scholarship boy journey from a working-class community in Compton, California to graduate school. I unpack my tensions associated with ideas around success and I try to tease out a way in which I can negotiate my own contradictions and frustrations with "rising up" within the constraints of dominant society and hegemonic notions of schooling/education and "success."

Chapter 3, "Home," explores the philosophical dimensions of "home" for Mexican-origin scholarship boys. Specifically, I explore how the working-class home of the participants serves as a life management system that assists them with dealing with issues of social class, alienation, and distance from their physical "home." As such, I theorize on spiritual, psychic, emotional, and cultural dimensions of home and its links to molding activist, academically oriented, scholarship boy identities.

Chapter 4, "Masculinities, Class, and Power," draws from masculinities research to analyze how Mexican-origin scholarship boys utilized a certain form of intellectual manhood as a coping mechanism when interacting with Whiteness in K-12 and higher education. Moreover, I center the role of power and manhood, and how their barrio roots provides them with culturally situated knowledge that they turn into empowered masculinities in the classroom.

Chapter 5, "Toward a Ghetto Nerd Framework," focuses on the gifted identities of Mexican-origin scholarship boys. I specifically outline a framework by which to understand the giftedness that is often overlooked when unpacking the identities of working-class, Latino male students. The Mestiz@ Theory of Intelligences (Carrillo, 2013) is an extension of Multiple Intelligences Theory (Gardner, 1985) and the portraits of Mexican-origin scholarship boys illustrate how educators, policymakers, and other interested stakeholders can imagine a way out of dichotomous street kids vs. school kids notions of working-class student identity. MTI also provides one of the first, published, intelligence frameworks that is specific to the identities of high achieving, low SES Latino males.

Chapter 6, "Revisiting Richard Rodriguez," provides final thoughts related to how this work connects with and in some ways, extends the work of Richard Rodriguez. I intend for this chapter to be primarily narrative-driven as I work through my concluding reflections on scholarship boys.

Headwind/Soulwind

In sum, what follows are narratives of struggle, change, loss, and gain. I am reminded of Deloria's (1999) words: "Western civilization seems clear, orderly, obvious, and without possibility of reform primarily because it defines the world in certain rigid categories" (p. 4). Schooling in the United States is very much ordained by a particular very order. The Latino males in this book navigate this headwind even amidst melancholic desire to evade, change, escape and play in the river far, far from the metanarratives of the "American Dream" and bounded notions of "success."

Music. Print. Thirst. Kindness. Boldness. Resistance. Community. Love. Justice. Vulnerability. Genius. Elegance, humor, and the tragicomedic. It has taken me many years to narrate and compile and bring together this beautiful struggle. There were so many people that I had to meet, so many graveyard shifts in graduate school while eating Ramen Noodles, so many travels into the ultimate hotel and community, the soul. I just me a kid at Walgreens in full skateboarding gear – he told me that he went to X-Games, Austin. I grabbed a bag of pens and thought: I am inspired by the artists of space bending who navigate a world of guarded and often limiting interests. Perhaps this kid has dreams that will end in joy or disappointment, or something much more messy. Still, I am reminded of Richard Rodriguez's (1992) reflection:

> Who is more right – the boy who wanted to be an architect, or his father, who knew that life is disappointment and reversal? (Is the old man's shrug truer than the boy's ambition simply because the shrug comes last?) (p. 230)

What follows is not an answer, but a testament to the polemics of how some barrio boys achieve academic excellence in ways that heal and hurt. It is very much: an American story.

CHAPTER 2

LOST IN DEGREE[1]

The following essay was written during my time as a graduate student at the University of Texas at Austin. Upon writing this essay, I was not aware that I had sent it out for publication. The private pain I was experiencing, apparently somehow moved me to submit this to a journal. It was a couple months after I submitted this piece to the Journal of Latinos and Education (JLE) that I realized that my scholarship boy story was something that some readers could relate to. Upon its publication in JLE, I received dozens of emails from scholarship boys and girls from across the nation. Those emails continue to trickle into my inbox. To all of you, thank you for the community we have built and for sharing your stories with me. Also, I begin with this essay because it introduces key themes of loss, academic success, and identity in ways that provide context for the ensuing chapters in this book.

> This is a reflection essay that posits the issues of identity, education, and social responsibility on the shoulders of a dream gone wrong. Beginning in the violent streets of south Los Angeles, a young Chicano boy (me) becomes addicted to the word and inquiry at age 5. He follows the tenets of society, seeking upward mobility and happiness via higher education. In spite of being raised on welfare, he is able to study and make it all the way to PhD study. Then tragedy sets in; or an epiphany that should have came many years before. How much have I lost? Why do I not want to pursue the academic track anymore? Why do I feel invisible amidst visible characters engaged in daily living? Ultimately, will I get a second chance and will I be able to go back home?

In the summer of 1994 I left Compton, California, in search of myself. I left to the University of Michigan with the blood stains of my cousin Fidel, as he lay in the front yard of my home after his murder a few days before my 18th birthday. My father, the alcoholic, the human being that I was supposed to look up to, was in shambles. My mother, as she counted her food stamps, told me, "Con cuidado, estudia mucho."

I am 30 years old now. I am in a vacuum; pigeonholed into a library and the prose and diction of academia. Innocence lost, again. I look at the student loan debt I have incurred and the fumes of futility. A hostage, looking into how a role model became disillusioned by the mural he painted.

This is a reflection on the academic journey of a Chicano PhD student. Me. I start here, in the latter stages of my PhD program as I reflect on the I, on the past, on tomorrow, and on the word. Dislocated by the marginalization of a law-abiding human being, I write with the understanding that rubrics formulate salaries; rubrics speak to who gets published. This narrative is the delivery of something from a place that a CAT scan cannot trace; I give you the well of my grandfather's wisdom, with the angst and pain that goes back before the cavemen began to talk about multicultural education.

My sincerest apologies go out to those who read this on a bad day; your day may get worse. Actually, though, I really hope that lessons come from this and a record of the here and the now as I see it.

Every time I open a book now, I feel like my innocence has been lost. I have climaxed in some ways. I am about to graduate with a PhD in hand. But I do not want to be a university professor anymore. You see, I am not a deadline writer or in the mood to shake a few dirty hands for the sake of upward mobility. I came to this planet Earth March 9, 1976, born in south central Los Angeles, with a notepad in hand, free to create lyrical artwork on a moment's notice. I have lost myself. I have lost the culture I am now paid to explain. I have lost my sense of solidarity with accepted knowns. I live one paycheck away from homelessness, and I cannot see my children as often as I would like to; this PhD dream molded my divorce. In a schizophrenic state of mind I search for capitalism's department of reparations. I run. I read and run. I am no longer a Latino. I am invisible to others and myself; I have crossed intellectual, psychological, and emotional borderlands with a ferocity and speed that not even Jeff Gordon can catch at the Daytona 500.

I am restless, the manifestation of the Chicano movement's ideas on empowerment; I was highly influenced by this literature. Yet, my Aztlan entails that I attend conferences with intellectual midgets who patronize in umbrella terms the needs of my mother who works in a sweatshop and the agony of my father's search for redemption. I am America. I am raceless, spaceless, humbled by academia's harsh lesson: I do not have a home.

How is it that a young and courageous boy with a massive thirst for knowledge reaches the pinnacle of his intellectual mind map and then realizes: I should have never taken this route? How do I deal with my discontents? In search of truth and deliverance I ended up enslaved by my own theories. I am disowned by the proletariat and at odds with the bourgeoisie. I am graded to the point of an ink-based hemorrhage. My solidarity is now with the ethical standard of those who do not write but speak from within.

Henry David Thoreau's Walden (1854/2004) framed my most recent hollowness. As we strive to reach ambition, our trajectory ends up in submission. We dig our own grave, when all we had to do was enjoy and cherish the wind's PowerPoint presentation and the ocean's waves of classic reads. Truth, knowledge, and happiness lie in that which you are not trained to think of as important—you step on it every day and ignore it on your way out of the house.

My conscience is clear. I fell in love with school at age 5. I am now about to break up with school as we know it. Additive models of inquiry should be not confined to semesters, literature reviews, conferences, and vengeance politics. If we would have listened to our mothers, we would have known a long time ago that the Statue of Liberty looks east because this country was made by them and for them. We enjoy subtle moments of joy all while questioning our part in the exploitative assembly line.

Like dead men walking, I join the pack and push my way through as I scream at the men in three-piece suits, and then I disagree with a Chicano scholar on his or her version of tomorrow. It could just be that every time I write I mourn the derailment of what could have been. Imagine just 40 Latinos, men and women, of all ages and socioeconomic backgrounds creating their version of Levittown. Our master planned community. Imagine. It never happened.

The sun is so beautiful in Austin. In my heart, in my head, I fish on a puddle that has 5 inches of water. I read article after article all while teaching high school kids about the importance of a college education. Am I lying to them? Is eating a churro at the swap meet, practicing for a family member's quinceañera, and taking days off from work so I can hang with my pops in the front porch more important? Is that true knowledge, truth, and deliverance?

The sorrow is overwhelming sometimes. I have missed too many birthdays of loved ones. I have my mother suffering from diabetes and I provide little counsel. I speak of my mestizo roots all while shopping at Macy's for a Kenneth Cole shirt. I do not do drugs or smoke cigarettes, yet I am under the influence of intellectual carcinogens—a chest pain ensues. My renaissance is right now, a rebirth; I am a born again invisible man. Now, somehow, I am going to have to frame what is next and what role academia had in my disappearance.

I want to pay for a one-way ticket to ride on a dirty and crowded Greyhound bus back home. Can this PhD education allow me to go back? Do I know what that looks like? Can I be ok with it? Where are my Veterans Affairs benefits? Vietnam in the classroom. This journey is violent and full of terrorists deploying a jihad on my senses.

It all started innocently enough. Go to college. Get a degree. Then I realized I could get two degrees. Done. Now, I thought, would I be able to have what it takes to get a PhD? With this degree, I could change the world, myself, and the plight of the disadvantaged. I have changed. A lot. And I have left behind the most important people in my life for the arrogance of 12-in font and the enzymes that salivate during a game of cerebral ping pong. I should be jumping up and down. This is my heart bleeding before you; these missteps immortalize the diction riding the railroad tracks that caused an accident. I am off the tracks! I am off the tracks! Nobody cares, nobody looks, and everyone thinks that I have "made it."

To the Chicano intelligentsia everywhere, I would like to say a few things. Have you been able to put on SPSS not only the data for the article that you want to publish, but the data that correspond with the impact of your actions on the most disenfranchised strata of our community? If I read your article that is not saying a lot. I am supposed to read it. It is ok to be a conscientious scholar, but keep in mind the limitations of our claims. Is it time to formulate a new model for training our young Latinas and Latinos? Or have macroscale forces beyond our control such as inflation, real estate speculation, stagnant wages, and globalization created a reservation system that makes our ideals impossible to implement on a grand scale? The issues are more global now; the layers are thick, the starting point is not the notepad.

I feel like I was born today. Working in reverse, I am going to try to finish my last few courses and write the desperation so that I can receive my doctoral degree. I will also go back to Macy's, but this time I want to see if they sell cut-up jeans as shorts, Casio watches instead of a Movado, and the shirts my cousin used to let me borrow. I want to find the missing clothes of yesteryear. And in that, maybe, just maybe, I get to start all over when I walk out. But if the clothes are no longer there, I hope that you will remember that it is important to hold on to that which you may never get back.

NOTE

[1] This essay was previously published as: Carrillo, J. F. (2007). Lost in degree: A Chicano Ph.D. student's search for missing clothes. *Journal of Latinos and Education, 6*(4), 347–350. Reprinted by permission of Taylor & Francis LLC (http://www.tandfonline.com).

CHAPTER 3

HOME

> I have taken Caliban's advice. I have stolen their books. I will have some run of this isle.
>
> (Rodriguez, 1982, p. 1)

It was love at first sight. With words I could go home. All the smog in Los Angeles, California filled up the sky with the music to build my mind and soul. But it was then, as a small working-class Chicano kid that was never able to slam-dunk a basketball that I began to understand the power of "home." Academic achievement, dignity, words, and this place, "home," all connected somehow. The feeling is intense. The language of home sees a *gringo* attempting to tell the "truth" on PBS (Public Broadcasting Service). It names assimilation. The language of home has aluminum foil all over the *carne asada.* There are contradictions and a dynamic set of exchanges between childhood bike rides and mainstream schooling contexts. Becoming an academically successful student has a painful poetry and clarity. These tensions are layered with tragicomedic tensions: how many "high achievers" remember trying to bring a bilingual parrot from Tijuana, Baja California, Mexico to Los Angeles, California?

So, it is not about escaping community, but taking its "best practices" with you. Taking its soul with you. Taking its struggle with you. You utilize the precious knowledge that you got in spaces of nurture and tension to intervene in an unequal world. Home is embodied. Home then, is a spiritual and psychic space, a library much more insightful than those in the Ivy League. Knowing and being on the side of one's working-class home is a commitment and a stance in solidarity. The barrio nerds in this chapter utilize home as a set of memories, as the root impulse and the informer that leads to humanization and inspires their ongoing struggle to fight for social justice principles. This is an uneasy search and link. It is, painful and often, healing. By connecting with home, we see our friends, our families, our "culture," and our love for the innocence of a more holistic time, even if it is sometimes somewhat romanticized. We love and miss the "block." The hunger for the past makes the scripts that we are living open to critique and reimagining.

Historically, marginalized communities all over the world have articulated a desire for finding, claiming, representing, and/or remaining connected to "home." Chicana/os speak of "Aztlán," some rappers allude to the area codes that are linked with their communities of origin, Palestinians have a symbolic and literal struggle over complex questions germane to "home," and graffiti artists often mark "their territory." The Mexican-origin scholarship boys in this research also express a similar yearning. There is a messy, hopeful, and sometimes despair-oriented search for the "source" and meaningful residence.

Leaving one's working-class "home" to pursue one's educational goals creates all sorts of tensions and reflexivity for Mexican-origin scholarship boys. This departure is not merely a physical separation, but premised on philosophical and symbolic changes. Internal voices attempt to resist "capture." In other words, the smells, aesthetics, values, and classed experiences of past and present develop an argument of sorts. In fact, from Hoggart (1957), Rodriguez (1982), and Carrillo (2007, 2009), we can discern that there are very few concepts as central to their scholarship boy analysis as the connection to their "home." This research extends these ideas by looking at "home" as the epistemological, ontological, spiritual, and philosophical compass that elicits strategies and standpoints that assist in negotiating the race, classed, and gendered expectations of K-12 schooling and higher education. Through a series of discourses revolving around the "education for success" mantra, Mexican-origin scholarship boys grapple with the philosophical dimensions of what it means to depart from a home in a working-class community and attend institutions of higher education, which embody complex intersections of race, class, gender, and ontological (and epistemological) hierarchies.

Schooling involves a complex ideological and emotional-spiritual entanglement between working-class origins and the middle and upper middle-class spaces of academia. Not only did the Mexican-origin scholarship boys interrogate everyday experiences, but they also examine the larger issues about how "home" informs their evolving understanding of history, truth, knowledge, success, and their private and public identities. Their approaches to these issues embodied a hybridity which parallels with Anzaldúa's (1999) notion of mestiza consciousness. This differs significantly from Rodriguez's (1982) binary of public and private self. It appears that searching, remembering, and examining the eclectic dimensions of home aided in breaking when necessary from the ontological demands of the *mythic terrors of the enlightenment* (Horkheimer & Adorno, 2002).

Are scholarship boys "Always Running" like Luis J. Rodriguez (1993)? Are they exiled "citizens" immersed in the poetics of the ontology wars?

How do the sociocultural, philosophical dimensions, and what Vygostky (1978) implicitly frames as the "historical self" around the polemics of "home" engage a dialectic with what Feinberg (1995) suggests is one of the core questions in the philosophy of education: what should count as education? The philosophical dimensions of "home" for Mexican-origin scholarship boys are also informed by Dubois's (1903) infamous question: "how does it feel to be a problem" (p. 7)? As subaltern students of color, living and studying within Western, Anglo, Protestant, middle (and upper middle) class, and Cartesian discourses on schooling, they attempt to place and name their location (in part) by "looking back." Part pragmatism, part romanticism and existential angst, the search for meaning rides heavily on how "home" is imagined.

Is enlightenment nothing more than totalitarianism as Horkheimer and Adorno (2002) argue? Mexican-origin scholarship boys grapple intensely with this very question. Interestingly, the spiritual and ontological shortcomings of the enlightenment seem to incite a hunger for "home." This became particularly strong for the graduate students that are part of this study. This is part of the nostalgia of many scholarship boys. Richard Rodriguez (1982) dropped out of his doctoral program after imagining home in certain ways. I also wrote the essay, *Lost in Degree: A Chicano PhD student's Search for Missing Clothes* (Carrillo, 2007), after tapping into my reflections and memories associated with my working-class "home." The "original" scholarship boy, Hoggart (1957), wrote about how scholarship boys get information in the schooling world that does not fit the experiences of their working-class upbringing. Maxine Green (1995) reminds us that Western notions of reason can be a dominating ethos. Even though they are raised amidst the linear and hyper-masculine tropes of modernity, Mexican-origin scholarship boys appear to embrace a reflexivity largely informed by their reference to "home."

GRADUATE STUDENTS: MARIO AND ANTONIO

Mario: Homeless Amidst the Enlightenment's Tower of Babel

According to Richard Hoggart (1957), scholarship boys are uprooted and anxious primarily because they are removed from their working-class origins by pursuing "success" in traditional spheres of schooling. For Hoggart, social class and the accompanying cultural architecture of a working-class environment makes scholarship boys uneasy in mainstream spaces of higher education. Much of Hoggart's portrait of the scholarship boy examines how "home" as a sociocultural and emotional place of origin, informs the feelings and choices of scholarship boys.

For Mario, the "uprooted and anxious" feeling is so strong that he had to leave the city in which his PhD program is located. He went "back home" to his working-class community even though he had yet to finish his coursework. He took a bus and flew in for classes, so that he would not have to be around the university and the city on a continual basis. For Mario, he wrestles intensely with a *double consciousness* (Dubious, 1903) that encompasses a frustration over seeing himself through the imposition of dominant class ethos. This philosophical aesthetic is embedded within the discourses of the university. He took all sorts of measures to do whatever it took to be "far enough" from the symbolic and literal violence he felt at a predominantly Anglo, middle class institution of higher learning. In fact, he told me that he never studied at the university library. He would go to the libraries of other local colleges to avoid being sucked into what he refers to as *the puppet world of academia*. But after two years of living in his hometown again, he says:

> *Oh my God, you know, I do feel homeless. I would agree with that 100 percent. It is a metaphor for knowing where you are from. Your real home. It's about knowing that you moved away, so far.*

Mario goes on to examine how leaving his hometown to pursue higher education lead to culturally subtractive experiences.

> *My identity, my value system, my conscience, this makes up my belief systems and morality. All of this got disturbed, actually erased to the extent that I became homeless. Bro, there is no way around it, I pretty much got erased by going to college.*

Caught between leaving and going back "home," the identity of "homelessness" and the consistent use of the term "erased" centers much of his analysis. This in many respects encompasses Dubois's (1903) notion of African American attempting to find a true and holistic self-consciousness. In fact, in part, it is through a *double consciousness* (Dubois, 1903) that Mario goes on to draw many of his conclusions. Mario's assessments are stunning, especially in the light of scholarship that implies that racial minorities from low SES communities arrive at "success" if they can make it to college, graduate, and enter into the world of middle class public life. Mario clearly projects a melancholic embodiment of the anti-Horatio Alger narrative. The question arises though: can you ever really go back home? Hoggart (1957) provides his own analysis:

> He cannot go back; with one part of himself he does not want to go back to a homeliness which was often narrow: with another part he longs for the membership he has lost, he pines for some endless Eden where he never was…he both wants to go back and yet he thinks he has gone beyond his class, feels himself weighted with knowledge of his own and their situation, which hereafter forbids him of the simple pleasures of his father and mother. (p. 232)

As Mario speaks about "home" he often speaks about the innocence of the past with a saddened tone. Moreover, he also positions the intimacy of his working-class home and the values of his community of origin as having a more "authentic" grasp on ethics and "true knowledge." Mario's philosophical assessment of his working-class community of origin drives his anxiety, a sometimes contradictory dialectic of hope and angst, and furthers his varying degrees of liberation and oppression.

Thinking about my own scholarship journey, I reflect on the day I drew a violent conclusion about my schooling journey: it was all partially based on a myth. I began to deconstruct how children of promise are indoctrinated in our barrios to pursue academic success, supposedly leading us all on our way to some notion of utopia, U.S.A. I can recall all the graphs and presentations in high school that argued that going to college meant higher earnings and all sorts of other economic benefits. What was never mentioned, are the spiritual and cultural aspects of ambition through the metannarative of Western notions of "making it." I got divorced along the way. Also, the knowledge at top-tier universities began to look like a fabrication of a few elite storytellers. So, as I reflect on the "myths" germane to my experience, I urge Mario to expand on the role of formal schooling in his life.

> *It all goes back to the success bullshit. Success is a measure by those individuals which it was meant to be successful for. Education is the key to success? We want to believe that. But, it is all a myth. The reality is that you have to sell yourself.*

Perceptions of "home" through this level of concientization encompasses a dialectic similar to Anzaldúa's (1999) *mestiza consciousness*. By reflecting on his hometown and the discourses that took him away, Mario does what Anzaldúa (1987) frames as a revolutionary act: "…participating in the creation of yet another culture, a new story to explain the world and our participation in it, a new value system with images and symbols that connect us to each other and the planet" (p. 103). He also embodies a *spiritual mestizaje* (Anzaldúa, 1999) that ruptures certain norms. Still though, he does not appear to develop a tolerance for ambivalence, ambiguity, and contradiction, cornerstones of Anzaldúa's notion of *mestiza consciousness*. Also, unlike Rodriguez (1982), Mario does show a desire to somehow remember home as he processes the present, seeking to embrace some ownership over his version of life, education, success, and meaning. Hence, he does embrace some notions of hybridity whereas Rodriguez splits the public and the private self, arguing that public success in middle-class life is worth the cost of losing aspects of one's cultural origin. While Rodriguez "remembers" the past, Mario attempts to reclaim it.

For Mario, his ontological conflicts interact with the often unexamined shortcomings of the enlightenments foray into implicit claims of neutrality around ideas germane to certain notions of progress, schooling, and success. Horkeimer and Adorno (2002) argue that "...enlightenment itself has been reduced to animistic magic" (p. 7). This magic resembles Mario's analysis of the "myths" associated with his scholarship boy experience.

> *After many years of reflection, I know now that there is no way I can finish my PhD without losing so much. How much will be left of me when I turn it in? Slowly, subconsciously, every time I took the next step up in the academic track I keep erasing more and more of the real me. And that is why I am so frustrated. Sometimes I just go look into other fields imagining an escape from all this. Your essay, it really spoke to me you know. It connects with the subconscious. It really speaks, especially as it relates to deconstructing the struggles of self, of identity. It really is about asking: what is the purpose of life now? What is my real purpose in my life right now, at this crossroad? What your essay*[1] *does, is tell that story of how you come into all of this for social justice. I did. Then, though, you begin to deconstruct the world as it really is. You begin to indict the myth. The myth is that you will produce a masterpiece. The myth is that you will go to these universities and professors will sit down with you and guide you as true compatriots and take us from where we are to what will be instead of the reality which is who we are to who they want us to be.*

There is a core sense of disappointment as Mario examines his narrative. His life story draws us into a journey from the barrios to what is considered one of the top institutions of higher learning in the nation. He often brought up Saul Alinsky's philosophy of addressing the world as it is, versus how it should be. As Mario navigates his double (Dubois, 1903) and mestiza consciousness (Anzaldúa, 1987), he engages in a critical and dialectical assessment of his predicament. According to Mario, the American Dream and mainstream notions of "making it" are not easy to accept for he realizes that his culturally situated identities are often at odds with dominant society's' expectations. He told me that around the end of his bachelor's degree is when he was starting to draw these conclusions, with more clear proof in graduate school. He shifts into a startled incoherence, as he examines his assessments. He at once knows that formal schooling provided an introduction to certain ideas and forms of literacy that he enjoys and benefits from, but at the same time, he cannot confidently feel poised in his belief that he can find a home in the traditional nomenclature of academia and middle-class life. Mario tries to straddle a *double consciousness* (1903) but finds little comfort in his sense of resistance. His counter-stance to accepting any elements of middle class life strain his sense of meaning making. This incoherence is explained well by Sennet and Cobb's (1972) analysis of two working-class men that were deconstructing the impact of social class mobility in their lives:

> Knowledge through formal education they see as giving a man the tools for achieving freedom-by permitting him to control situations, and by furnishing him with access to a greater set of roles in life. As things actually stand, however, certified knowledge does not mean dignity for either of these men; indeed it is the reverse, it is a sham. What needs to be understood as how the class structure in America is organized so that *the tools of freedom become sources of indignity.* (p. 30)

For Mario, this indignity is experienced every time he feels separated from working-class rhythms of "home." He has the cultural capital to enter many spaces and perform well, yet, the act of participating in the rituals of middle-class public life in the university stuns him into an often dark depression of sorts. He tells me:

> *I don't understand how these white boys just sit on the ground you know, at the library at the university. Like what fuck?! You know it's their university, their country. They are so comfortable. We can't do that. We are always on guard. Before I sit down to study, I find a place where I am really by myself. I can't just lie down in the main walking area like them. I feel their presence, I feel their cultural codes, I feel their oppressive ways. I know I may be over acting. But the anxiety is there, so it's very real to me.*

Interestingly, like all of the scholarship boys in this research, Mario loved to go to the library since he was a child, but he despised going into the library of his own university because according to him it had certain floating signifiers of power and privilege which made him uneasy. Mario often told me about working with well-known civil rights activists. He was quick to point out that his journey from his working-class home led him to see the world as "it really is." His drive for engaging in activities that address social justice was scarred and altered by the many negative experiences he had with institutions and people in power. Many of these people were idols of sorts to him, but they fell short, for they were according to Mario: *unethical and self-serving*. Mario begins to tell me about the frustration he has with middle class life.

> *I was drawn into the facts. The world as it really is. I decided to work towards shaping this world for the better. But then, you get into this middle class space, school and life in general, and you realize that you have a paper due in two weeks. The committee then has to approve what you write about. Your story only makes sense if you can explain it to them. My story, in some crazy way, becomes their story. They have to know it or else I don't exist. You see that sick relationship? You have to get the consent of the powerful. To do this, I have to become more and more like them. I have to follow their rules.*

Higher education was implicit in the domination of Mario's working-class ontology and epistemology. He despised having to defend his sociocultural self and the knowledge structures he brought with him to the university. Mario was angered by the fact that his cultural capital and funds of knowledge had to be approved by a committee of professors. *It's hegemony you know*, Mario would often say. The linear and hyper-rational expectations of middle class life distort Mario in all sorts of ways. As he addresses frequent feelings related to being "homeless," he begins to remind me of what Hoggart (1957) calls a "classless intelligentsia." According to Hoggart, scholarship boys become classless at some point. He contends that this happens after scholarship boys realize that they cannot "really go back home" and do not feel poised (and happy) in the middle-class world of academia. Richard Rodriguez experienced some of this tension and so did Richard Hoggart. Unlike Rodriguez though, Mario really does want to "go back home" at all levels. He does not believe that this desire is an exaggerated and overly romanticized impossibility. Also, very different from Rodriguez, he does not concede that middle class life was "worth" leaving home or losing some of his connections to his culture(s) of origin. So he is stuck in a conundrum. Although Hoggart's (1957) use of the term "cultured" is somewhat flawed (he really means, "high" culture), he addresses some of Mario's ambiguity: "Talent brought you into that circle, you belong to it, but…you are drawn away, and you waver between cultured people and lodgers, vis a vis" (p. 234).

I remember a friend once asking why I had put so much weight on the value of college. He reminded me that "most people" go to college to just get a good job. He encouraged me to not "over analyze" it. He suggested that I just get a "good job" and move on. It was very difficult to explain to him that schooling was a vehicle that meant more to me than just a place where you go to eventually make lots of money. My own scholarship boy journey, connected in many ways to Mario's own trajectory. Mario and I imagined our communities as places we loved, but in need of some repair and assistance. We believed that doing well in school would give us the tools to help end poverty, discrimination, and unequal access to opportunity. In some ways, I think we both felt "chosen." Why else were we able to enter mainstream spaces of success and not most of our friends? The answer, for sure, is complex. But, we gave up a lot to see this journey through. In some ways, crossing the *cultural capital line* feels unethical and flawed. Our own lives feel chocked by a long narrative of propaganda. In the essay I authored, *Lost in Degree: A Chicano PhD student's search from Missing Clothes* (2007), I pondered:

> How is it that a young and courageous boy with a massive thirst for knowledge reaches the pinnacle of his intellectual mind-map and then realizes: I should have never taken this route? How do I deal with my discontents? In search of truth and deliverance I ended up enslaved by my own theories. I am disowned by the proletariat and at odds with the bourgeoisie. (p. 348)

Mario's philosophical manifesto or running strand clearly is, in part: his academic journey was shaped by a set of myths that took him away from "home" and then left me stranded. Like Rodriguez (1982), he was in part moved to gain "culture" through learning; culture in the sense of acquiring the master's tools to reimagine and redesign the master's house in a more social justice orientation. The search for the purpose and meaning in his journey is exemplified when he stated the following:

> *I cannot ever say again that college is where every poor Mexican from the 'hood should go. I cannot say that without shooting the person with*

> *a lie. This hurts, this school thing. I am crying right now, you know. What happened to the beauty and integrity of the barrio in me? It's kind of gone. Love, real knowledge, I had that. Used to have that.*

After many years of reflection, he senses that that he was a certain type of prisoner (indoctrinated into the western, middle class, Protestant, Eurocentric schooling cave), finally freed in some respects at least, by escaping the ideological darkness that he frames as the Horatio Alger narrative of upward social class mobility by way of the scholarship/schooling system.

A nostalgic search for the Eden where he may never have been now drives Mario to look back and remember who he was, who he is now, and how to articulate his next steps. The philosophical dimensions of his reasoning borders on varying degrees of existential angst and liberation.

Gloria Anzaldúa's (1999) *mestiza consciousness* also taps into philosophical questions similar to those of Mario. For Anzaldúa, a new consciousness comes from the pain and incoherence of embodying a hybridity that injures and liberates. Mario contends that college injured the symbolic and literal manifestation of his memories germane to his working-class "home." Like Anzaldúa, Mario is attempting to repossesses the cultural, historic, and spiritual dimensions of his being, interrogating his interaction with the "myths" germane to his schooling journey. This emotional and intellectual scaffolding is in part aimed at re-imagining the racialized, classed, and gendered "man of reason." Mario is critically conscious of the intersections of varying discourses in this *Tower of Babel* – the American university. Drawing from Anzaldúa (1987), a *mestiza consciousness* informs Mario with a restless psychic and emotional interplay, often with immense feelings of insecurity.

In some ways, Mario imagines a utopian community is right around the horizon. He sometimes suggests that this place can be acquired through careful analysis, reflexivity, and "wiser" choices. Mario did go back home. As I was starting my interviews, he relocated back to his hometown. He said his goals were in part:

> *Giving back, going back to the roots. Maybe I can rekindle old networks. With some of the new information I got, maybe I can do something there. Maybe. I just need to get the hell of this university world. I can finish my PhD from where my heart really is.*

Mario appears to be developing a new consciousness, one largely informed by his views of "home." Though he often implies that he is homeless, he actually embodies an emotional, intellectual, and cultural shelter that clearly is a certain notion of "home." This perspective on home provides a compass, helping to guide his actions, feelings, and choices. His perception of home is often in a dialectical conversation with his schooling experiences and his working-class community of origin. Cleary, Mario's analysis in part resembles Rodriguez's (1982) assertion that "…education is a long, unglamorous, even demeaning process – a nurturing never natural to the person one was before one entered a classroom" (p. 68). Yet, unlike Rodriguez, Mario wants to reclaim some version of what he deems as a working-class authenticity by retrieving some elements of what he perceives as the "homeland." This cathartic struggle reminds me of my own journey. I got on a dirty and smelly Greyhound bus in south central Los Angeles in 1994. My *tio* (uncle) Chito waved a good-bye. My backpack had quarters in the front pocket because my mother said that loose change is important, just in case there is an "emergency." My destination was: the University of Michigan at Ann Arbor. I felt so uprooted in a psycho-cultural and spiritual way, that I left the university after a short stay. Mario is presently struggling with a similar battle. His imagined and physical home have provide new insight, sources of strength, and inspiration to finish his graduate study and become a better person in the most holistic sense. Mario is presently exploring new ways to be deemed, *an educated person.*

Coping Strategies

What strategies enable Mexican-origin scholarship boys to cope with their psychic and emotional distance from home across time? Drawing from Mario's philosophical assessments of "home," he appears to approach this question from a couple of directions:

1. Physical relocation to his hometown.
2. A continuous critical reflexivity.
3. A certain detachment from claims of success and knowledge production related to the academy's expectations of doctoral students.
4. Service to his community of origin.
5. Philosophical dimensions of home.

Mario moved back to his hometown. Even though he struggles with the limited access he has to books and other resources by being a few hours away from his university campus, he shows no signs of going back. Drawing from a revisionist take on Dubois's (1903) *double consciousness*, Mario appears to have more confidence in negotiating a working-class identity and the middle class cultural capital of his doctoral program by moving back to his old neighborhood. He comments:

> *I was not about to become a program, a software program. Here, I can go to the liquor store with "buck-shot" and other real people from the neighborhood and then go home and work on my theoretical framework. I can dip in and out on my terms into both of these worlds.*

Going back to his hometown helped Mario feel connected to his cultural origins in some ways. He motioned that this critical piece was missing from his life when he left to go to college. His love and affinity for giving back to his community is intense. He spent many years as undergraduate student working as an activist to provide better schooling opportunities for all the youth in the area.

After writing this section, I began to write in my reflexive journal. I was very moved by Mario's story. Here is a free-verse that was inspired by Mario:

> The lost sheep. Lat-inos. His-panics. Raza. The Muslims painstakingly arriving at Mecca. Chicanos claiming Aztlán. Jerusalem and Palestine and the disagreements over land and time, stories, history. At the advent of the 21st century, where modernity and Western Philosophy dripped and dripped and took and gave me something all while pouring cement on the city streets….these blood stains, these heartaches, my R & B song after the ballad is no longer on the radio…even after Obama won, the scholarship boy…in search of home as heaven and Earth collide with string theory and its discontents…civilization and its moral argument. I hear. I hear. I love and feel my way through even after I run out of quarters. My brothers, like Icarus, flying away, with the fall in sight. The Hohokam possibly imagining our rise. With Henry David Thoreau, I write from Walden Pond, with St. Augustine, the existential demand drives me closer and closer to home. God and Plato, my mother and fear, the post-Puritan hope, the stagecoach in endless spiritual migration. A mortgage payment is not enough. From heaven, the decolonial search-light is created. I see. I will be. Home. Soon. I feel, therefore I am. Descartes just used his head. Even after immigration reform, home and dignity has to be pursued… across all borders.

Home. Kierkegaard's (2009) *Fear and Trembling* reminds us of the responsibility, faith, ambiguity, and loss that accompanies the human project. Like Kierkegaard's depiction of Abraham's journey, Mario is so far from home. His meticulous dedication to the scholarship journey isolated him and changed him immensely. Even after he moved back to his hometown, he no longer is *really there.* When Mario looks back, outside of the regrets, what can he claim now? In some ways, modernity is engaged with considerable discontents. Enlightenment liberalism and its request for the scientism of the soul – there alone, lies Mario, the Mexican-origin scholarship boy. Much of his conflict stems from the yearning for the poetics of the past.

Gloria Anzaldúa positions a lens to best understand Mario's philosophical take on "home." Anzaldúa (1987) stresses the connections between the mind, consciousness, and action. Anzaldúa (1987) explains:

> Knowledge makes me more aware, it makes me more conscious. 'Knowing' is painful because after it happens I can't stay in the same place and be comfortable. I am no longer the same person I was before. (p. 70)

For Mario, "knowing" affected his conscientization process across time. His insight is both "felt" and embedded in thought. He is able, albeit with much angst, to physically relocate and to use his cultural intuition and formal knowledge to continuously redefine himself and seek a more complex whole. This process is part of his *mestiza consciousness.*

Mario does exactly what Anzaldúa (1987) claims is a revolutionary act of self consciousness – he blocks certain hegemonic acts with a counterstance. This awareness and action draws its strength largely from how Mario imagines his community/home. Mario tells me:

> *You know, I am always splitting atoms of the soul. I know that I left something, now with this university shit, I have to go back in my heart and know who I really am. I split inside all the time, it hurts, and then I realize I do it to fight back. To fight back against all this made up stuff. Even when my professors think I am being lazy or lacking dedication, it's really just me taking the power away from them. I have a say you know, I opened the pandora's box and the hype exceeds the reality. Now, it has to be on my terms, even if it means not getting this PhD.*

While Hoggart and Rodriguez analyzed their scholarship boy experience at the level of dualities: working-class vs. middle class, private self vs. public self, Mario embraces a break from any dichotomy. His intersections of consciousness and being are informed by multiplicity (engaging his raced, class, gendered, and historical selves) and the courage to form something new. In this way, Dubois's (1903) *double consciousness* does not have to consist of a permanent separation of two or more worlds. Instead, a sense of hybridity can claim all spaces, good and bad, at once, in one body and psyche. His memories of home cause severe emotional suffering, but it also incites a desire to interrogate every action and idea. While the positivistic and progress discourse of enlightenment liberalism urges a static (and a sense of fulfilled arrival) definition of self, Mario embraces the possibilities of seeking to find himself, yet, willing to take the risk of never having all the answers. Irresolution, or what Anzaldúa (2002) calls the *bridge,* may in fact be the space that always changes, a *nepantla* state of consistent transition, shift, and cross over.

There are many tongues spoken at the *Tower of Babel.* Mario is expected to write a certain way, behave a certain way, and "move up" in the world in a certain way. There are so many ways to celebrate his "epic" rise from the barrios of a U.S. city where very few go to college. After many years of intense reflection, Mario points to the beauty in all of us, found, at the original place of departure. *Home*. Working in reverse, he reminds me of my own words and reflections, which I published in the *Journal of Latinos and Education* (2007):

> Performing for Protestant metanarratives
> Weber and his slanted mirror
> And my day is over
> I get to break the code of silence
> Not believing in the Bering Strait myth
> I am reciting the emotional manifesto
> Embracing the altruistic civil war
> To get educated
> On my terms. (Carrillo, p. 347)

I now turn to analysis of Antonio's interactions with "home."

Antonio: Let's Go Cruisin' While We Wait for Godot

Samuel Beckett's (1982) world renowned existentialist and minimalist play, *Waiting for Godot*, illuminates some of Antonio's core philosophy:

> Estragon: (chews, swallows). I'm asking you if we're tied.
> Vladimir: Tied?
> Estragon: Ti-ed.
> Vladimir: But to Whom? By whom?
> Estragon: To your man.

Vladimir: To Godot? Tied to Godot! What an idea! No question of it. (Pause). For the moment.
Estragon: His name is Godot?
Vladimir: I think so.
Estragon: Fancy that. (He raises what remains of the carrot by the stub of leaf, twirls it before his eyes.) Funny, the more you eat the worse it gets.
(skipping a few lines)
Vladimir: I get used to the muck as I go along
Estragon: Is that the opposite?
Vladimir: Question of temperament.
Estragon: Of character.
Vladimir: Nothing you can do about it.
Estragon: No use in struggling.
Vladimir: One is what one is.
Estragon: No use wriggling.
Vladimir: The essential doesn't change. (p. 17)

Godot's play goes on to explore the tensions associated with the search for meaning and explores the absurdity of life when one waits for "something" or "someone" to provide meaning or fulfillment. In Sartrerian type of existential allegory, Antonio also appears to be waiting for Godot. Similar to Hoggart's (1957) assessment, he does want to go back to his working-class childhood days but yet feels weighted by his ambiguous social class standing. He has a master's degree but does not have full time job that "pays well." Still though, he does live in a cookie-cutter middle-class home and says that he is *bored out of his mind in this fake world.* Antonio is centered on nostalgic memories of what he sometimes describes as an eden like childhood, one that he often contradicts by speaking of the poverty and urban decay in the places he called home. He reminisces:

> *We used to play with no shoes. Over there, the weather is usually always nice. I loved it. It was hard, money wise, but I was free. I did not have to sell myself yet. I did not have to get intoxicated by all this "work hard" crap. Those days were about exploring nature, seeing big things in little things. My imagination would run wild. I wish I could go back.*

Like Hoggart (1957), Antonio has an excessive "self consciousness," especially as it relates coming to terms the cultural and psycho-social consequences of his journey since he left the barrio:

Going from the barrio to college does not mean a whole lot to me right now. I thought that by leaving I was going to learn more. What I did learn was based on my search and desire to learn on my own. They said read one book. I read five. I added my own list. I feel like the hypocrisy of the whole thing is what stood out. These professors are suppose to be these supreme beings, but I found out they are no better than anyone else…I think now, that for a Latino, goals have come from the individual. Write it down, accomplish it, with or without the university's help. It's another Disney movie, it's a folk story to keep you around to not riot. It's all to not get you depressed. All these lines about making it, it's a twisted myth. You spend years looking for that making it to the finish line. The American dream is a fantasy. I mean, if it's about getting what you actually want, most people never get that. The American dream is a slogan like "Drink Coke." My dream was to own Lucas Ranch (film studio), my dream right now is to at least enlighten people with some of the stuff I have done. I am hoping I am not a total waste. Hopefully, somebody says they got something from my work. I am not done yet.

This type of analysis was consistently mentioned. Antonio wrestles with much pain and angst germane to his attempt to "make it" in mainstream society. From this analysis, Antonio has a nostalgic emotional and philosophical emptiness. His sense of being stationless, homeless, and just living a myth is sometimes paralyzing.

The warmth and source of strength he has remaining in his life is his look back at the first part of his life, specifically childhood. There is nothing about getting a masters degree that makes him claim that he "moved up" and achieved something of significance. Antonio reflects:

When I was child, I used to have a tree-house. Problems came, I just went back to the tree. Everyone had these big trees, even if you were poor over there. I felt the serenity. It was townhome living the way it was meant to be, up in that tree.

Childhood lost, childhood in utopian terms draws in a source of hope. Antonio spends most of his days at home, making home movies, reading, analyzing everything and everyone. Only by reflecting on the past, does he feel somewhat fulfilled. He did not get a career upon graduation, but instead got rejection. He could not land a job as a media technology specialist or get a shot at any film studio. In fact, he began to hear employers say: *we hire people with experience.* His university education left him with theory, but according to Antonio, *no practical experience to land some good job*. He has a restless air, often oriented towards his anger over going to college.

Valenzuela (1999) points out that a feeling of marginality among many Mexican-origin youth in K-12 schools is the result of socialization away from the community that one grows up in. Interestingly, this is an issue even among Latino scholarship boys like Antonio; those deemed to have earned the credentials that society deems as educational success. The Mexican-origin scholarship boy Richard Rodriguez (1982) addresses this conundrum as well:

> What I am about to say to you has taken me more than twenty years to admit: *A primary reason for my success in the classroom was that I couldn't forget that schooling was changing me and separating me from the life I enjoyed before becoming a student.* That simple realization! For years I never spoke to anyone about it. Never mentioned a thing to my family or teachers or classmates. (p. 45)

Thinking about the working-class past and the childhood home that is long gone, provides for provocative analysis of the intrusion of "education." Antonio also misses the intimacy. Antonio reflects:

> *You know, I miss eating by the tree in my hometown, yeah I was poor, but so was my neighbor and his neighbor. Poverty, we have to define it. I'm more poor now with an advanced degree. I didn't find a good job and I don't have a sense of community like before. College had artificial goals, I was forced to put all the outcasts together and call them my friends. You know, these guys with big dreams, but the university ignored us. I hate to say it, but now, we must think about how the barrio needed repairs, not departure. Some drug problems were in it, but we had beautiful things too, the cultural side. I can never be down for filet mignon, I want carne asada, and I mean this as a metaphor for everything else. I don't get it, you are born poor, then you to college, and you stay poor.*

Antonio exposes conflicted, contradictory, and painful questions about social class mobility and difficult philosophical questions around linear notions of "making it." Like Rodriguez (1982), Antonio misses the intimacy and rhythms of his working-class home. Now, stuck between a physical, cultural, and psychological departure from "home" and making sense of his new life, he battles with the ideologies that have him spending days wondering what went wrong. Carrillo (2007) also alluded to the consientization process of his scholarship boy journey whereby going from the barrio to graduate school resulted in a sense of incoherence due to the sense that utopia, "arrival," and success are complicated destinies tainted with complex intersections of reward and subtraction. Following the rituals educational success often times result in emotional and sociocultural dislocations that are difficult to synthesize.

Nonetheless, there are coping strategies, especially as it relates to how Antonio imagines "home" which help him address some of the uprooting from the barrio. I address this in the section that follows.

Coping Strategies

Antonio drives a car in a way which he says is based on where he is from. He states:

> *I hit the road low and slow. I know my roots, my Mexicaness, my city vibe. Shit, I put some Eazy-E on, and then just pull down the window.*

Carlos imagines his hometown as a place that made him "real" and "authentic," to him it is a region known for its dynamic, urban sense of self. Today he lives in a city he calls *a conservative, racist, shopper's paradise.*

To deal with the microagressions of schooling and its expectations, Antonio appears to use his memories around home in very specific ways:

1. Home serves a psycho-emotional place that grounds his identity in opposition to certain ideas behind middle class values and whiteness associated with college and achievement discourses. His perception of home draws from a *double consciousness* (Dubois, 1903) that encourages his search for multifaceted dignity and success.
2. The physical elements of home are also inspiring and important. He can always "go there" and feel like he is "somebody"

It is important to note that Antonio lives about 600 miles from his hometown. He often goes back, walks around, and uses this drive as a pilgrimage of sorts. He can claim, once again, his ontological center and identify where he was before entering public life and its demands. Antonio reflects:

> *I go back to my barrio, cause that is where people actually live to live. Yeah, we had drugs and poverty, but we also have humanity. I touch the ground, smell the air, take in the beautiful weather. I live in a little*

suburban home now, bored as hell, trying to pay the next bill and really not doing a whole lot.

So, "going back home," albeit with all sorts of nostalgic, romanticized, and contradictory elements, fulfills Antonio's total humanness. While Rodriguez (1982) went "back home" during his graduate school experience and then went on to pen his memoir, I sense that Antonio is looking to find that type of meaning making as well. Antonio is a filmmaker. His deliverance may have to come through a movie. He tells me:

Let's go together, to make a movie about the truth; about the ghetto, about brown men trying to make it. About how much we get charged at every step. And they wonder why we are the only ones that supposedly made it?

The idea of home has long been part of how many oppressed groups frame a sense of protection, prospects for renewal, and holistic notions of self. During the Chicano movement, Aztlán served to enumerate an actual physical place as "home" (the U.S. southwest). Antonio points to the role of barrio, as it relates to Mexican-origin scholarship boys, and its potent impact on the development of a dialectical philosophical identity. Within this reality, hurt, happiness, failure, and social debates on achievement get immersed within a critical debate whereby the working-class past battles the hegemonic, middle class expectations of the present. Hence, "reality" becomes negotiable. This phase of conscientization and negation of the schooling mobility process as an all encompassing and liberating dimension on all levels fosters tensions and new "truths." It is that tension, the past in battle with the present that gets him to say:

There are no easy answers except knowing that inside of us, we all have success. Who do we keep listening to? Whoever that is, we have to press mute.

Antonio is searching, ambivalently, for the belief that he truly is right. Inside of his detachment from metanarratives of success, he is poised to find his way *home.*

FACULTY: CARLOS AND DAVE

Carlos: Searching for Summer Amidst 'The Winter of Our Discontent'

In John Steinbeck's (1961) *The Winter of Our Discontent*, there is a poignant passage: "It is strange how a man believes he can think better in a special place. I have such a place, have always had it, but I know it isn't thinking I do there, but feeling and experiencing and remembering. It's a safety place – everyone must have one, although I never heard a man tell of it" (p. 36). That special place, the search for it, is something that moves and alters the psycho-emotional states of scholarship boys like Carlos. This Steinbeck classic has a special place in Carlos's schooling journey.

> *Winter of Our Discontent, upon reflection, was "assigned" to me unofficially by Luis Oberto (pseudonym), a raza educator in high school. This is the vato who was my high school teacher and more importantly, my AP/college prep teacher when I was in AP/college prep for one day. (Remember I left after a crazy kind of rejection of the possibility to be good at something – a straight negation). Bueno, total, I was talking to him one day and the vato (you know how we teachers are – drop names of books like fish hooks so we can see who'll take a look) starts talking about that I should read Winter. And then the cryptic motherfucker says: "Then come back and tell me what the talisman represents." Vato, I didn't know a talisman from chupacabras at the time, so I had to go look it up. (Most of my early books, at the age of 17, 18, are full of underlined words with the definitions in the margin.) After looking up the def, I jumped into a paperback of Winter. My jefe would trip out on me cuz I'd be up till midnight and up at 6 reading that libro. I remember trying to figure out white slang in the book. Skullbuster. (Tu crees, all this time and I still remember that.) I said "What?" Orale. Pisto. I get it and all that was a trip to me. I guess I liked how the vato treated me seriously. You know, it's a homeboy thing. So, in sum, I would have to say (and I'd love to hear your interpretation) that the book mattered because it was assigned in a time of crisis (I was trying to be somebody and was going about it all fucking wrong) and it was insinuated with an instruction that was more like bait. Luckily, I bit and he knew how to reel me in. But his mentorship, to exhaust the metaphor, was catch-and-release. The vato took me serious without believing all my bullshit.*

Carlos was an honor student for much of his elementary school years. Upon entering middle school, he began to suffer academically. From middle school onward, he no longer had the intimacy and care that that he felt as a child from the schooling site. He framed this transition as a violent time; he needed love and affection at school because at home and in his community, there were many physical and psychological threats to his development. Through the deficit thinking (Valencia, 1997) of teachers and school administrators, he was, in general, perceived as another low achieving student. This was a violent discourse change for Carlos. Nonetheless, Carlos maintained his intellectual curiosity and like many scholarship boys, spent long hours at the library:

> *The library was a sanctuary. A place to workout. A workshed for the mind. I was a four or five times a day library person. I would get one or two books to read quick and go back. At the library I could remember that I was intelligent. Reading there reminded me of that intense intelligence. I would just sit on the isle. I would also go to Seven-Eleven (store) and get those magazine subscription cards so I can get material to read.*

The word sanctuary often came up when Carlos and I talked. He was and continues to be in search of this sanctuary. This is a place of being, characterized by redemption, moral, spiritual, and intellectual success on his terms, and this is a place where he can engage in social justice issues with his own sense of legitimate contribution. In the library, with its eerie silence, you can look up and find the writers who you can "talk to" and expand on so much of the dire conditions in which he lived. There was domestic violence at home, little if any teaching at his school, and gangs fought for position at the schoolyard. Carlos wrestles with a *double consciousness* (Dubois, 1903) in some ways, as he negotiates the racialized, classed, and gendered domains of barrio life with the expectations of the formal schooling site.

So how does his working-class home inform much of Carlo's identity? For one, "home" is the place where the pain started. This pain is what elicits knowledge, memory, and emotional tropes of what he should do with his life.

> *Pain was central to my development. One of the number one things I remember as a child going to school a block away with my little brother, walking with my backpack when the night before we watched my father beat the shit out of my mother. Early on, I carried that memory. My brother was a lot more trusting. I would not easily be convinced by my father to get him to take us to school and stuff. We grew up in the barrio. You can tell with the Raza at the graduate level, the students, we can tell if they have been through pain, through just their telling of their stories. It is like a reunion with brothers and sisters you never met, when you see people that go through this stuff. You hear them and we draw a connection right away.*

Pain and its epistemological and ontological implications, informs the dialectical imagination and conversation with the working-class past. For Rodriguez (1982), his pain came not from living like Carlos amidst urban poverty. Rodriguez's pain, though quite impactful and legitimate in its own right, does not grapple with what it means to be a son of poverty and live the Mexican-origin scholarship boy life from what might truly be from the *bottom up* (though this research questions the idea that we do actually "move up" by advancing through the dominant narrative of "making it"). Hence, nostalgia, a salient trait amongst many scholarship boys (Carrillo, 2007; Hoggart, 1957; Rodriguez, 1982), has powerful implications. While Rodriguez used the knowledge that came from his reflections (he felt separated from the intimacy of his working-class past) as a graduate student to infer that losing much of his private self was a necessary loss to garner his "successful" public identity, Carlos does not agree with such a notion. Much of this stems from the fact that for Carlos, the pain started way back, as a child in the bungalows of marginalization, disenfranchisement, and barrio heartache. He explains:

> *To borrow from Mary J. Blige, I am a child of the 1970's, raised in poverty and sin. We grew up ill carnal and that is part of the home experience through and through. Any effort to edit or censor that is fruitless. And I think, upon serious and prolonged reflection, that dimension of home is what took me to Southwest University (pseudonym). Going to Southwest, or trying to go there I should say, the going there was contingent upon the acceptance letter, but the desperate trying to go there, anywhere else but Soledad (pseudonym for hometown), was fueled by the ill side of home. The same feeling I felt before leaving from Southwest is the same feeling I have right now, two years after returning...Home for me was a violent, dysfunctional, and traumatic. It was also efficacious and fulfilling, but the majority of the family's time here in the U.S., has been on the underside of the American illusion that each successive generation does a little bit better...*

The dialectical and contradictory aspects of home fulfill and yet punish the very core of what Carlos feels he deserves as he moves towards a space of healing. He mentions the "shadow" nature of going back to the physical home, where he "bumps into himself." In a very profound and metaphorical way, the barrio is visible in the way Carlos speaks, postures, and delegates his notion of academic fulfillment. The pain, ambiguity, and crossing between spaces of healing and punishment, earmarks the part of his identity that resembles a *mestiza consciousness* (Anzaldúa, 1999). Initially, Carlos wanted to leave "home" to pursue higher education (which he did) and now upon his return, feeling trapped and confused, it all earmarks the constant struggle for balance and meaning. He bounces off between the metanarratives of publish or perish and the barrio scholarship boy wanting to work for social justice and see life in more cyclical ways. His skipping around between the ideologies of spaces which are tainted with race, class, and gender tropes resembles Anzaldúa's (1999) poetic explanation of the mestiza:

> Because I, a *mestiza*
> Continually walk out of one culture
> And into another,
> Because I am in all cultures at the same time,
> *Alma entre dos mundos, tres, cuatro,*
> *Me zumba la cabeza con lo contradictorio.*
> *Estoy norteada por todas las voces que me hablan*
> *Simultamente.* (p. 100)

The dialectical interactions with home, as a moving, still, literal, and sometimes physical, sometimes emotional-spiritual space, provides the funds of knowledge by which Carlos makes sense of social stimuli in many instances. Carlos explains a relevant point:

> *For those who grew up similar to the way I did – there are few, the children who survived what the "War on Poverty" could not eradicate – we set ourselves apart and engrafted ourselves to one another. We represented vato. And I think it's tragicomic that we mindfully represented urban centers that were cruel to us. Pero alli esta donde los ombligos estan enterrados homie, straight up.*

As a self identifying Mexican-origin scholarship boy from the barrios of Los Angeles, I have many memories of the way poverty and gang violence created an emotional and cynical pain. Deep embedded in the soul, there was always a frailty to the idea that public policy and the America of the middle-class seemed to ignore me. In spite of the dark experiences in the barrio, the dialectical umbilical cord is very much linked to how Carlos imagines "home."

Hoggart's (1957) "uprooted and anxious" argument about the lives of scholarship boys fits well when understanding Carlos's experiences in academia. The uprooted social class tension was so strong that during his first year of doctoral study, he "took some pills" as he put it. Carlos was at one of the most prestigious institutions of higher education in the world and yet the aggressions of memories germane to the past pulled him into violent states of consciousness. It is the departure from "home" that poses an intense conundrum for Carlos:

> *Home makes you strong…distorts you in all kinds of ways, makes you ill-suited to the "surface" culture of the university….but there is a nagging question for those that come from where we are from tambien: Is the struggle itself – regardless of victory in the form of the PhD – something pyrrhic? Is the outcome of formal educational accomplishment too ambivalent to say, "Well, it was all worth it in the end?"*

It is this same question that nagged me. In *Lost in Degree: A Chicano PhD student's Search for Missing Clothes* (Carrillo, 2007), I confess:

> I read article after article all while teaching high school kids about the importance of a college education. Am I lying to them? Is eating a *churro* at the swap meet, practicing for a family member's *quinceañera*, and taking days off from work so I can hang with my pops in the front porch more important? Is that true knowledge, truth, and deliverance? (p. 349)

In remembering the past, a dialectical relationship with the present consists of a dialogue of being and synthesis. The past was not a utopia and earning a PhD did not deliver a prophetic punctuation. Consciousness and identity tropes wrestle with the discourses and assessments of past and present. The pain of the "winner" in the social class mobility trajectory rarely gets examined by the education literature. In my own scholarship boy journey, I in part concluded that I did not necessarily "move up" but instead moved somewhere else (culturally and in terms of consciousness). Rodriguez (1982) made mention of the nostalgia that brought him back "home" to Sacramento, California after years of obediently following the rituals of the celebrated scholarship boy. Rodriguez went on to make many choices that forever changed his life based on this dialogue between his assessment of his schooling experiences and his former "home" life.

Certain notions of home encouraged Carlos to complete his doctoral studies. He kept the authenticity of his working-class home as he sees it, without becoming a full- blown victim to the trappings of "remembering." He speaks to this effect:

> *We represented, often to our own detriment. I know vatos going on their 10th or 11th year that have yet to finish (doctoral study) because of this*

loyalty to a certain kind of Chicano representational practice. I have to respect that homie, for reals. But it's hard to watch. But I gotta respect that battle to not fold to this world.

Carlos negotiated his double consciousness (Dubois, 1903) as he wrestled with the memories of the past and still found ways to find meaning and "soul survival" at a mainstream institution of higher learning. This was not easy of course. During our interviews, he often hinted at the idea of *knowing alleys and dark places* on his graduate school campus that only he really knew about. These were places that he owned, in principle, spaces where he meditated and had psycho-emotional dialogues. Carlos found tremendous strength in the working-class consciousness he possessed from a long life of struggle. Still though, he forges a mestiza consciousness (1999), where he refutes dichotomies and boundary setting identity politics. He knows that the past is part of him, so much so, that he moved back to the general area of his upbringing. But, he claims a right to his evolving today. That is, he is a professor, and he contends that this is becoming a space where he has achieved a certain aspect of his synthesis and happiness. As he told me, *I always wanted to do this, teach, read, become a professor, this is me.*

Carlos grew up in a major urban center (he teaches at a university in his hometown). His dialogue and interaction with "place" enumerates how public space becomes a cognitive, emotional, spiritual, and political argonaut. While in graduate school, *he spit* (expressed comments with a certain urban, lyrical urban code) his intellectual prowess with home in mind. He made this clear to me when referring to some of his Latino faculty and peers as engaging in the assimilationist process of becoming what he referred to as *coconuts* (white-washed people of color). Now, upon returning as a professor to his former neighborhood, he takes the city bus and writes extensively about his interactions with the place he believes to be his psycho-spiritual residence. He draws strength and intellectual flexibility and inspiration from the cement, the grit, the ups and downs, and the struggle of working folk in his hometown.

Carlos became a PhD student through the intersection of a mentor's constant push in his undergraduate institution and his meeting with a well known critical pedagogue at a ski resort (the irony behind this location made him laugh). After borrowing money from his grandmother, he drove off many miles from his home to meet one on one with this professor at the resort. A couple of calls later (with this same faculty member) and after taking care of other intermediary details, he was admitted at a prestigious tier one university located in the southwestern United States. What is particularly moving and stunning about this journey is that Carlos entered his freshmen year of undergraduate study because of a *bike ride.* He rode his bike in his early twenties to the local university which he has calls *the worst university on Earth* and from a little hill imagined himself taking classes there. From that little hill, holding onto his handlebars, Carlos thought about the prospects of becoming a university student.

How do the philosophical dimensions of home explain his awkward stumbling towards the university classroom? Carlos stressed the fact that he knew he was off the scale "smart." He was well-read and referred to libraries as "sanctuaries." But, he was stuck in public schooling spaces that labeled many of the Latina/o students as "dumb." The negativity associated with this labeling required a lot of self-reflection. Approximately two years after high school graduation he made it over to the hill, imagining himself as a college student. He did apply, got admitted, and earned mostly A grades. It was easy for him. He is a smart scholarship boy, continuously wrestling with the ethnocentric gaze of the systemic panopticon.

For scholarship boys like Carlos, social class does setup what Sennet and Cobb (1972) refer to as a contest for the pursuit of dignity. The right to "be somebody" is in many ways dictated by the expectations of the middle and upper classes, which in the U.S., are also often people from non-ethnic minority populations. So in this struggle to put oneself on par with those supposedly "above us," the scholarship boy renders his struggle an ideological battle with discourses on achievement. The "injured dignity" (Sennet & Cobb, 1972) that comes from race, class, and gender marginalization sets off a unique journey. This life course is engulfed within the liberating and violent dimensions of history, ontology, and the politics of common sense. In the polemic quest for acquiring the Bourdeian notion of *distinction* or "at least" public acknowledgement of "brains," the brown body and soul realizes that in a racist and classist society such as ours, dignity becomes something that has to be consistently fought for. That is why "home" is so important. The neighborhood, the working-class beginning never asked of the scholarship boy to become something else. The discourse was premised on the now and the struggle for survival. Tainted with contradictions and pain, freedom and suffocation, the barrio of his youth, for Carlos, always will be home.

It is interesting to imagine my journey and that of Carlos as a complex exercise of desire and struggle. The dialectic with the dreams associated with the partial goal of moving into another social class and "opportunity space" is vested in the process Bourdieu (1984) explains quite well:

> The dialectic of downclassing and upclassing which underlies a whole set of social processes presupposes and entails that all the groups concerned run in the same direction, toward the same objectives, the same properties, those which are designated by the leading group... competitive struggle is the form of class struggle which the dominated classes allowed to be imposed on them when they accept the stakes offered by the dominant classes. It is an integrative struggle and, by virtual of the initial handicaps, a reproductive struggle, since those who enter this chase, in which they are beaten before they start, as the constancy of the gaps testifies, implicitly recognize the legitimacy of the goals pursued by those whom they pursue, by the mere fact of taking part. (pp. 163, 165)

For Carlos, there is an ideological movement from home to university, back home, and in a continuous dialectic of becoming. While his peers were immersed in gamesmanship of barrio life, he switched between the schooling machine in its formal corpus and his love for hanging with the guys. Where did this desire come from? Carlos, like myself, was immersed with a wrenching thirst for pursuing his thoughts in the college arena. The challenge of going "over there" to where the "smart people go," a place where low SES youth of color rarely go (the university), provided a challenge. Carlos reflects:

> *For better or worse, Southwest University (pseudonym) became home. Not the only home, but the new home. It had its own pedo, but it was mostly the site where I had to work on the psychological mierda (shit) I brought from my hood...I feel that my time at Southwest University was like a prolonged moment from the Piri Thomas book, "Down these Mean Streets," that part in the book where the vato climbs to the top of the projects just to shout, "Hey world, I am somebody!"*

Fundamentally, the philosophical dimensions of home for Mexican-origin scholarship boys are immersed in Mike Rose's (1989) argument whereby he suggests that the push for choice or authorship of our lives as students in U.S. schools interacts with "what lies at the base of education – to be tapped or sealed over or distorted, by others, by us" (p. 240). The morphing of consciousness and memory elicit melancholic and triumphant moments of euphoria and dangling. There is: a dialogue of infinite longing.

Coping Strategies

Coping with the microagressions of his race, class, and gendered identities along with the mobility discourse and racialized and classed spaces of higher education requires an intense reflexivity and synthesis of what Carlos calls: *mierda* (shit). From this sociocultural and sociopolitical *mierda*, Carlos drew a firm conclusion recently. The journey, his journey, is immersed in *ambivalence*. Moreover, he has decided that that is ok. What Baldwin (1985) calls, "the price of the ticket," is the nagging question that sometimes destroys scholarship boys. For Carlos, there are some specific strategies used to cope with the microagressions of higher education and the mobility discourse in general:

1. Coming to terms with the price of the ticket
2. Reframing success
3. Learning from the dialectical relationship with *home*

Carlos explains his views of irresolution and contradiction:

> *The outcomes of obtaining a PhD are ambivalent. Perhaps I have said this, but maybe I have been feeling it more persistenly over the last year, recognizing it as a permanent facet of the Chicana/o (or maybe only this Chicano's) mind. That's all I can say vato – ambivalent outcomes. Como, you are a modern subject because you are well aware of the cost, but you do not agonize about it anymore, you are stoic. Chicano stoicism mas o menos. Puro contradiction and I think (and I think much like our foremother and fathers – Anzaldúa, Alurista, y so forth. You gotta be cool with it).*

The idea of being cool with it, reminds me of what I had trouble doing when I (Carrillo, 2007) elaborated on my scholarship boy journey by saying that I speak of my Chicano roots all while buying a Kenneth Cole shirt at Macy's. This sense of ambiguity and class consciousness wrestling with the acculturation aspects of middle class socialization requires some meaning making and coming to terms with contradictions. Carlos contends that social class mobility and his identity as a Chicano from the barrio of a working-class community have finally resulted in a hybridity he can live with. Anzaldúa's (1999) notion of *mestiza consciousness* entails a similar aim, where irresolution and ambiguity become forces that one accepts. Carlos now forges a new consciousness as he learns how to cope with the tensions of contradiction and ambivalence. Carlos addresses the issue of success and "making it:"

> *My PhD was just made worth something because I helped my tio get his Social Security disability. He always been slow and I love him. I am now a God in the familia. But sabes que vato? That's the problem. I'm just the sobrino, not no God, not the Social Security slayer, ni madres, simplemente a homeboy who somehow made it. (I guess I made it, I got a firme job, I help a grip of Raza and white folks tambien – simon, I unequivocally made it G, I'll hold to that). Imagine if he had lost, I would have been the one who fucked it all up. And it aint that either. Como the scale of me within the family has been lost. And still nobody knows what the PhD is in. That matters, that hurts me, eso si me llega hasta el pinche alma. For me it quaint no more that familia just knows I'm educated. I want them to know what I do. I hate them and love them vato, for reals, no exaggeration on that, I love them and hate them and I hate myself for doing that.*

Again, Anzaldúa (1987) reminds us of this type of hybridity and contradiction. Mestiza consciousness (Anzaldúa, 1999) is in fact related to the way Carlos has to wrestle with the contradictory forces of his life. The ambivalence of "making it" in the context of the Mexican-origin scholarship boy means that some family members will get lost in translation. Moreover, the acculturation aspects of the journey create feelings of guilt and shame. Carlos has struggled to define his journey as authentic and beautiful in spite of the contradictions. In fact, ambiguity and ambivalence is what make the process so rich and rewarding. Only now, as a university professor, is he coming to terms with this identity.

The dialectical relationship between the schooling journey and Carlos's working-class home have provided new ways to imagine success as well as allotted meaningful spaces by which to come to terms with the losses and gains associated with his scholarship boy journey. There are many gaps and frustrations he may never clean up. Yet, Carlos's examination of his past has brought him into a new consciousness. Home is where his heart can heal. Slowly, he is starting to feel that he is finally home. Once you draw this philosophical inference, you can go and be anywhere, and still know that home is something one can define and organize en route to personal fulfillment. Home is not utopia or a feeling that warrants a sense of unquestionable arrival at some dominant notion of success. Instead, in the case of Carlos, home is where the mind and the soul get a voice, aiming at some negotiable sense belonging, arrival, and wholeness.

DAVID: HOME AS A STRUGGLE

Chicano identity, regardless of physical location, is something David takes everywhere he goes. Struggle is home, specifically, the struggle that stems from his advocacy which is largely informed by the ideas that were generated based on his experiences as a working-class barrio boy. David explains: *so home to me has been where I have lived at that time of my life. But my Chicano identity has remained a constant throughout my life.* David adds: *In my case, Chicano is a political identity. I am Mexican, Mexican American technically without the hyphen.* David attended public schools in the 1950's and 1960's in a major urban area located in the southwest. His experiences speak to the marginalization of Chican@ youth, with the constant tracking of brown youth into blue collars jobs. He recalls an experience that triggered his evolving critical consciousness:

> *At age 15, I started thinking about things. My white counselor asked me what my father did. "He works with his hands," I said. She said it was a very honorable profession, I should follow in his footsteps. At that time Mexicans and blacks were tracked into woodshop and stuff. I told my father about it. He told me to tell that white bitch that you will not work with your hands but with a pencil.*

David stayed close to his community to attend graduate school so that he could not only feel closer to familiar surroundings, but so that he could also be part of what he did become: one of the leaders of the Chicano generation. He adds: *I was close to the community. So that it was my source of power. I was an intellectual warrior.* Perhaps, an offer at Stanford, where he got accepted seemed lucrative, but he told me that it was not a place to pursue the independent model of research (he said it was based on the traditional apprentice model) and it was also a space that did not feel like home. *I went to Western University (pseudonym) because it was close to the barrio. This way I will be able to survive.* Western is a very prestigious, small, and private university in a middle class neighborhood. Yet, it is also very close to a several barrios. A few of these barrios were places David used to call home as a child and adolescent.

Now, as a professor emeritus, he reflects on his hometown as a place that among many positive memories did elicit doses of pain. He tells me: *The memories (of home) remain painful so that they continue to play a central role in the way I act within my own family life.* These memories serve as ontological pieces of information which guide his continued activism and healing process. Moreover, this dialectical and reflective aspect of remembering home, rekindle new pathways by which to become a mentor to students and live a life of dignity. While Rodriguez (1982) sought out "home" while he was a graduate student and found a debilitating incoherence, David looks to the past to inform "clearly" what he feels are ethical, critical, and spiritual takes on his most pressing contemporary dilemmas. Among the most important examinations of his past came when he visited a therapist. This came only recently, he reflects on this:

> *Being a child of violence, I was as a kid beat up by my stepfather. I was a battered child. The streets, that was about more violence. I really wanted to break that cycle. I had posttraumatic syndrome. My experience was from the streets and barrio. I did not know that until recently. I was in prison you know too. Then, in the Chicano movement it was a different kind of violence, had death threats all the time. So until now, to this day, I have still have stress and anxiety. I studied Buddhism and meditation for a lot of years. I went to counseling and therapy. I was not diagnosed until one therapist finally did it, she said these are the same symptoms of posttraumatic syndrome.*

This was a powerful moment. I self-diagnosed myself as having some form of posttraumatic syndrome. I told David of my connections to this assessment. As a freshman at the University of Michigan, I recall friends asking me why I turned around so much when I walked. After growing up in neighborhoods where I often feared for my safety, I had a hard time "just being a student." Sleeping was quite difficult as well, for the silence of Ann Arbor, Michigan's nights were unbearable; I had to hear ambulances and helicopters to feel balanced. So, hearing David talk about posttraumatic syndrome reminded me about my own scholarship boy journey. David made mention that he still struggles with this. The process by which his past has affected his life is quite significant.

Interestingly, unlike Hoggart's (1957) and Rodriguez's (1982) assessment that scholarship boys cannot resolve the tensions associated with the uprooting aspects of upward social class mobility, David points toward a different assessment. His lifelong commitment to his community has provided a space of strength and stability, in spite of the occasional sense of ambivalence and painful memories. David's involvement in the Chicano movement and his continued support of Latino youth stems from the way his upbringing has instilled a certain mindset and purpose within academia. As we discussed some of these tensions of class and race as it relates to Latino scholarship boys who struggle in higher education, he expressed the following sentiments:

> *My advice to graduate students is that you just have to have faith in yourself. Be mindful that is just an academic exercise, nada mas. Es todo! It's just about developing a skill as a researcher. Y alli se acaba el pedo. Who you are, its not about you, put that on the side. It's just about getting a certification. The real work is after, when you graduate. Then you have more freedom and the chance to rewrite your work or do other work...don't put your soul into it. They want you to fall victim to that. You have to say, fuck you, fuck that and fuck them! You have to do the work you have a passion for. Don't do it for the job or career. Be what you want to be, find the passion within your work.*

The existential angst and sense of meaningless that Hoggart (1957) and Rodriguez (1982) connect with scholarship boys plays out differently with David. Or, better yet, as Carrillo's (2007, 2009) ongoing work on Mexican-origin scholarship boys suggests, the existential and nostalgic incoherence may be part of a stage that elicits a conscientization process, leading to new pathways for healing and becoming. David stands up against his own university's hegemonic discourses and has lived a life where he has been able to put his vision into pragmatic results like his involvement in creating Chicano studies programs at the university level. The existential dimension of the scholarship boy may in fact have been a critical piece of his identity at some point, but now, he has taken some agency related to those feelings. So, as his life shows, "looking back" is a powerful tool for empowerment. An existential angst does not have to play out as a stop sign. David moved beyond that, at least in large part, providing hope for other Mexican-origin scholarship boys who feel too uprooted to make sense of the journey.

Unlike Hoggart's (1957) notion that class-consciousness is stripped to the point where the scholarship boy feels classless, David has a clear, pragmatic, and dialectical relationship with the various *classed* spaces he inhabits. This reminds me the African American scholarship boys like Cornell West and Michael Eric Dyson who have maintained what appears to be healthy links with their working-class roots. David contends that the battle over authenticity and connections to the true self is based on how we articulate the idea of "compromise:"

> *My advice is that you never want to allow the institution to define you. We all have to make compromises. But, these are small compromises. We have to play the game. It's the only game in town. In the context of survival, it is what it is, but this is not about redefining who you are. You never should make profound compromises about your integrity, of who you are to be accepted. You make people accept you for who you are. I tell folk, you don't have to love who I am, but you have to respect me. I disagree with you, but I respect you as a colleague.*

Rodriguez (1982) argues that redefinition of the public and private self is a result of the long and unglamorous schooling journey of the scholarship boy. Leaving the intimacy of the working-class home involves an assimilation process that Rodriguez finds unbearable and painful. Although he confesses that the costs of losing an intimate link with the past was worth it, he nonetheless makes clear his irresolvable nostalgic existentialism. David suggests that a mestiza consciousness (Anzaldúa, 1999) can set you free in some way. Accepting the contradictions and ambivalence of the process of "becoming somebody" through formal schooling, enacts new spaces and possibilities. David's sense of class consciousness draws from his working-class home of origin, but he does not see his scholarship boy journey as eliciting an unbearable price and loss. I can still sense the "pain of the winner," but he moves towards internal dialogues of lifelong struggle as the best indicator of success and commitment to social justice.

Coping Strategies

I start this section by putting citing what Hoggart (1957) suggests is the tension and outcome of the scholarship boy journey:

> He is clever enough to take himself out of his class mentally, but not equipped, mentally or emotionally, to surmount all the problems that follow. He is denied even the 'consolations of philosophy,' of acquiring such comfort as there is, in part at least, from assessing his situation. Even if he achieves some degree of culture, he finds it difficult to carry it easily, as easily as those who have not had to strain so much to get it, who have not known like him the long process of exploitation of 'brains'.... (p. 234)

In my estimation, Hoggart is framing culture as cultural capital and discussing the transition of consciousness into middle class social mores.

What Hoggart poignantly points out is the incoherence associated with the tensions of assimilation and cultural change. What he fails to account for, nonetheless, is how some scholarship boys do have "philosophy" to lean on. This philosophy draws from how home is imagined. Moreover, this philosophical stance provides a vision by which to draw strength. This is particularly true for David, in that he organizes his dialectical approach with his working-class roots as the identity process of authoring a space of coherence and meaning.

According to David, *there is no distinction between private and public.* This is a different take on assimilation from that of Rodriguez (1982). David says: *I need to be who I am.* The public and private selves are constantly in a process of shift and change, crossing boundaries that are not static or ordained by some absolute law of behavior. It is this voice and positionality that that allows David to teach at one of the most prestigious, whitestream universities in the nation, while still maintaining a certain sense of cultural and class solidarity with his working-class past.

It is also important to note that David is in the latter part, as a professor emeritus, of his scholarship boy journey. After many struggles with committees over tenure and as a child of barrios that were known for their extensive violence, he examines his narrative as an accomplishment, never easy, in negotiating the genuine prospects of claiming the complexity of the sociocultural self. He starting teaching in higher education in 1968 and became a pioneer in the field of Chicano studies. For David, straddling the "uprooting" that pained Rodriguez (1982) consists, in part, by coming to terms with contradiction, and thus embracing a *mestiza consciousness* (Anzaldúa, 1999), whereby he wrestles with the gains, losses, compromises, headaches, and triumphant tropes of his scholarship boy journey. For David, home informs his choices and solidifies his role as an activist Mexican-origin scholarship boy.

SUMMARY

Closing Thoughts on "Home"

> Instead of pulling together we Calibans had all descended into our own spaces, taking the bus home every chance we got. –Junot Diaz (http://www.newyorker.com/online/blogs/books/2014/04/mfa-vs-poc.html)

Mexican-origin scholarship boys in this research tapped into the contradictory and empowering dimensions of "home" to deal with the microagressions germane to schooling and achievement discourses. Memory and nostalgia are key forces in their development and bridges to their working-class roots. A mestiza consciousness spurs a survival hybridity of self; an identity that wrestles with the contradictions of social class mobility by means of formal schooling in the United States. Drawing from Anzaldúa (1987), Mexican-origin scholarship boys negotiate their mestizaje as a way of remaining flexible with the psychic and spiritual demands of Protestant, Eurocentric, and Western notions of schooling and success. Whereas Rodriguez (1982) felt compelled to negate the prospects of cultural hybridity as a source of strength and knowledge, scholarship boys in this research make no claims to the idea that they have completely resolved the tensions associated with cultural conflicts associated with schooling in the United States, but are all adamant about the role of "looking back" as a process by which they nourish the dialectical dimensions of the their identity. Rodriguez argued for the separation of the public and private self, hinting at the debilitating dimensions of his internalized oppression. The scholarship boy, Mario, makes a different assessment:

> *Chale man, shit is too much a veces. Neta though, I am cool, and I think being a Chicano scholar is learning to live with that shit (ambiguity and contradiction), it ain't easy, it's like sitting across the table and having café with a Panther. (That's what the puto Richard Rodriguez couldn't do.) Y si, el pinche gato goes for you too, lo tienes que domar – con palabras o golpes. Me entiendes vato?*

I have encountered many social scientists who suggest that these are futile, hyper-romanticized narratives of loss. A critical reflexivity has positioned the Mexican-origin scholarship boys in this study to defend themselves from many self-professed owners of their identity. This is a painful and contradictory act of counter-dialogue. Mexican-origin scholarship boys studied and embraced many of the ideas of Western thinkers. I would argue that this is not a particularly bad thing. What remembering "home" in certain ways does, is help Mexican-origin scholarship boys enact empowered stances on what has been lost due to their academic success. Home also serves as literature review that helps them theorize on the blind spots of Western notions of schooling, knowledge, truth, beauty, and success.

Home appears to have a physical, spiritual, emotional, symbolic, psychological, cultural, historical, and political identity. Home starts their journey. Leaving home encompasses a complex set of assessments associated with views on success, education, and social justice. But, they never really "leave home." The scholarship boy Richard Rodriguez (1982) admits that he had denied the past as he hurdled through his lauded academic journey, only setting up the inevitable and painful interaction with his memories of childhood and adolescence. The scholarship girl Laura Rendón (1992) contends that home goes with her everywhere she decides to go. In the end, Mexican-origin scholarship boys engage the philosophical dimensions of home as the ontological and epistemological "residence" that guides perspectives on assimilation, knowledge, schooling, and life in general.

In the end, we also can trace the Mexican-origin scholarship boy experience to the history of Mexican-origin people. Home in many ways becomes the "unhomely" (Babbha, 1994), a fragmented identity embedded in gain, loss, ambivalence, contradictions, melancholy, and moments of optimism and clarity. This hybridity is rooted in Mexican and Mexican American history. Hybridity has been the result of multiple forces, including occupation, conquest, and dispossession. The Mexican American War and Conquest of Mexico, are but two key historical precedents that point to the long journey and battles against empires, the imposition of new myths, and the uneasy struggle over often not being allowed to pursue a path of self-determination. Going to college in the U.S. is deeply immersed in this legacy. And remembering "home," provides a last gasp, or one key form of critical agency to rename self, life, and the larger architecture related to being educated on one's terms.

NOTE

1 Mario is referring to the essay, "Lost in Degree," which is found in Chapter 2 of this book.

CHAPTER 4

MASCULINITIES, CLASS, AND POWER

…Cause the boys in the hood are always hard
you come talkin' that trash, we'll pull ya car
knowin' nutin' in life but to be legit
don't quote me boy 'cause I ain't said shit…

(Eazy E)

INTRODUCTION

School is a battlefield. All too often, Mexicaness operates within a discursive set of performances where students are classed and racialized as being at a "low level" in comparison to Whites (Betttie, 2003). Yet, the discursive, classed, racialized, and gendered performances of Mexican-origin scholarship boys contest this claim. Carlos once told me that he *loved servin'* (in this context, this is a metaphor, loosely defined, in this instance as: putting people in there place). I remember thinking that I enjoyed that same performance. The performance entails not only a demonstration of "smartness," but also encompasses the strategic use of certain standpoint/ social location (Latino, working class, male) to inform the listener about their blind-spots and lack of critical nuance on certain issues. A somewhat similar type of discourse is also prevalent during some rap battles and at the basketball court in many urban communities. Also, there is something astonishingly relevant about the aforementioned quote by the infamous Compton "gangsta" rapper, Easy E. Are Mexican-origin scholarships from the '*hood* (barrio) "servin'" as an embodied positionality against any person or institutional ideolog(ies) which may be "talking trash?" In the act of "servin," are they in fact not stealing a car (in reference to Easy E's quote), but "pulling" as in "decentering" anyone or anything that claims to have a stronghold on truth, knowledge, class consciousness, the body, or values? Is this a survival and/or empowerment mechanism inherent to a certain type of "male, barrio-centric ontology" for Mexican-origin scholarship boys? The label of "trash" may be linked with: the hegemonic university, peers who may appear to have "sold out," and the plethora of microagressions against the brown body, psyche, and spirit in a highly racialized and classed space such as a research one university (where all of the scholarship boys pursued graduate study).

While Latino masculinities amongst urban youth has often been theorized by looking at supposed pachuco postures of deviance (Paz, 1985), resistance against school norms and academic expectations (Foley, 1990), and within dimensions of how machismo may or may not be a cultural trait (Mirandé, 1997; Baca Zinn, 1982; Anzaldúa, 1999), few studies have explored the role of "performing smartness" amongst academically successful urban Latino males, like Mexican-origin scholarship boys.

A startling literature gap remains, one that has largely failed to include the voices of openly *sensitive*, Latino organic intellectuals (e.g. Mexican-origin scholarship boys in this research) who perceive knowledge acquisition as the process by which to become a more mature and well-balanced man. In deference to Octavio Paz (1985) and Richard Rodriguez (1982) Mexican-origin scholarship boys suggest that men of reason can be *real men* and *extremely intelligent*, while not assimilating into all of the constructs of middle and upper middle class perceptions of the *reasonable* and *civilized man of letters.* We can walk with an uneasy air (Octavio Paz despised this about Chicanos) and successfully perform in middle class spaces while holding on to much of the working-class past (an act Richard Rodriguez said was completely irreconcilable and Pierre Bourdieu failed to capture in his work on social reproduction of tastes, social class, and life chances).

The scholarship boys in this research express manhood in relational terms and use *masculine strength* in the name of social justice. Their "ghetto nerd" (Diaz, 2007) masculinities consist of maintaining a certain working-class, homeboy aesthetic while remaining excellent students (somewhat different from Diaz's more "geeky" conceptualization of the term). To this end, unlike much of the research (Ferguson, 2001; Willis, 1977) on working-class male students that designates unique and distinct characteristics to nerds and street kids, this research expands on this work by illustrating how Mexican-origin scholarship boys merge both identities. In other words, in some ways Mexican-origin scholarship boys are *vatos*, homeboys, and "keep it real" all while achieving academic excellence.

In this chapter, I will examine the cultural production of the gendering process of Mexican-origin scholarship boys, in part, by drawing from Connell's (1995) three-fold model of masculinity: (1) power, (2) production, and (3) cathexis (emotional attachment). Power will be examined through strategies that Mexican-origin scholarship boys use to "serve" hegemonic ideologies and structures and examinations into how these practices shape a "brain-centric" intellectual manhood. Production, unlike Connell's (1995) emphasis on capital and division of labor, is analyzed through the contested productions of truth, success, knowledge, and "making it." Cathexis consists, in part, of the emotional attachment to representing, honoring, and advocating for discourses, knowledge, and other aspects that reflect a commitment to their working-class communities of origin.

Finally, I will now examine the role of masculinities as it relates to Mexican-origin scholarship boys.

David: I Am a Fighter and Warrior

David often used the word "struggle" in our conversations. He referred to himself as a *fighter and warrior.* His historical lineage and life experience, very much points to the accuracy of this assessment. He is the descendant of someone who fought with Pancho Villa. He made me aware of this during one of our face-to-face interviews. He was proud to point out the role of struggle and fighting for justice that runs through his bloodline. David, like the Mexican-origin scholarship boy Richard Rodriguez, was inspired to use knowledge for some empowering end. However, unlike Rodriguez, David positions Antonio Gramsci and his *Prison Notebooks* (1971/2000) as core ideas and influences that shaped his views about how Mexicans and Chicanos in the United States (barrio residents in particular) live in a colonial setting. It is his intellectual positionality, one that has been fermented over years of self-analysis, activism, and a multitude of other experiences, that has encouraged him to not adhere to what his mother told him to be like: *humilde* (contextually defined here as humble or meek). He told me: *all the Mexicans who were being nice were being stepped on.*

David engages in a very deliberate act of contestation, challenging the status quo in any of the sectors of his life. He recalls walking with chains to protect himself from neighborhood gangs as an adolescent and later committing to the Chicano movement and critical theorists to re-negotiate, reimagine, and contest the hegemonic notions of knowledge and justice. In essence, "in his taking possession of knowledge" on his own terms, he is redefining the role of the *reasonable man of letters.* According to Mirandé (1997) "the reasonable man is not driven by passion or emotion but by logic and reason. He is not impulsive or irrational, but analytical, cool, detached, and calculating, and always reasonable" (p. 13). Is a Chicano scholarship boy like David a reasonable man? Considering the racialized, classed, gender norms of academia, David stands outside of the traditional tropes of the *learned and reasonable man.* In fact, he is often asked by the security guards at a campus garage why he is parking in the faculty area. The security guard cannot phantom the prospects of a Latino male teaching at such a prestigious university.

Unlike Paz's (1985) view of Pachucos, David's barrio-centric posture and positionality is not an aimless identity. Instead, David uses what Hoggart's asserts of the scholarship boys' central defining character, "brains" (he says he always knew he was a *smart Mexican*) as his vehicle for disrupting Eurocentric (and any other hegemonic constructs) notions of being an academic. David mentioned that he refused to live for the tenure process and that his commitment has always been to serve his community. He was proud to mention that his career shows a lack of interest in publishing just for the sake of adhering to the tenure track's code of behaving like a good academic. David rarely joins groups, he prefers the independent, self directed journey to truth. He reflects:

> *I rebelled against the old boys network. I was never was part of that and never will be. A lot of Chicano scholars continue to operate from the old boys network point of views. I never wanted to do that. I have always been a loner, to this day.*

During the interviewing process, David continuously reminded me of his autonomy and his role which is to: *speak truth to power.* To this end, he was very critical of many of the men involved in the Chicano movement because of their sexist views and he also questioned their role in becoming part of any established system. David is not affiliated with the two party system (Democrat-Republican) but instead chose to become an independent. He also seeks independence within academia. He eloquently explains:

> *Everybody (Chicanos) wanted to be part of the Democratic Party. That was one deal. I never put them down. But I have done a lot of critical talks about the two party dictatorship…I wanted to be my own academic and continue my own work for the independence of my mind. Our work has to be in the interest of the oppressed to create organic intellectuals.*

Hoggart (1957) asserts that part of the gender socialization for scholarship boys consists of isolation. He frames working-class youth as largely hanging out, outside in groups, while scholarship boys have to find the way to acquire isolation (to "study"). There is a certain type of insider-outsider negotiation that becomes central to their identity, a difficult process of masculinity shaping. David fits within this general observation, but also expands on Hoggart's view by asserting manliness as an identity that struggles to reshape and fight in the name of the oppressed. It becomes less about "I," like Rodriguez (1982), and more about "we"—we, the barrio, people of color. It is also stresses the role of using male privilege to contest patriarchy, racism, and classism. David's dissertation topic, choice of graduate school, and path as an academic can be defined as an act of resistance within and outside of the system.

In contesting the structure of academia at the ideological level, David does *take a stand.* Willis's (1977) study of the working-class youth positions the *lads* as working-class boys who are not agency-less. They perform deliberate acts of resistance against middle class constructions manhood (much of this embedded in the hidden and overt curriculum and achievement expectations). In the resistance effort, channels for social class mobility are in fact cut off in some ways. For Mexican-origin scholarship boys like David, the working class, racial-ethnic subjectivity also creates a tension, but he stays within the system (in part), where he performs very well academically, and uses his "brains" to question static notions of gendering, knowledge, and everyday aspects of one's life course. David has never been simply: "anti-school." His manhood encompasses a more complex toolkit for engaging oppression in a dialectical process. In a manner similar to my own experience, I recall thinking the following as a middle school student (paraphrasing):

> *A man fights back, a man does battle against oppression, but dropping out of school will not help me become a "cool," or strong "macho man." If school is the place that will help develop the mind, one day, I will use all this information to reshape this society in a way that helps people that look like me.*

This self-analysis was important because it was a position that was looked at with a suspicion. My working-class father sometimes despised my over emphasis on "reading" and my peer group was part of me, yet "not really me," because I went to the library after school and many of them refused to do their homework. David struck me as a sensitive, spiritual, extremely reflective, and a complex person (not to mention, someone gifted with the art of inspiring the listener). And it is these characteristics that forge an alliance with Anzaldúa's (1999) request for a *new masculinity.* In David's assessment of hypermasculinity, he mentions the following:

> *At first I was part of that. You don't think about it, you have to be a macho. It's the way it is. For some reason, by all the criteria I should have been a misogynist. My father beat up on my stepmother. All that patriarchal shit. Maybe it was something in my blood, I just didn't feel*

cool with it. When I tried to be a real macho, it did not make me feel good. Guys would talk about their conquests, I never did that.

David approaches classical liberalism's perspectives on diversity in the university as faulty dimensions of pursuing authentic justice and equity. Bloom (1987) is notorious for envisioning certain Eurocentric ideas as being cornerstones to the truly educated man. To David, the ontological and intellectual blind spots of this assessment require a stance of revisionism. To this end, masculinity, and his quest for power, are centered on having *his own voice*. He elaborates:

The problem is that the academy is an institution of the state. Some go uncritically into this. Some say: I am going to make it big and be a vice chancellor. I was one of the first among us to be offered to be a chancellor. But I said, "why do it?" Given the nature of the institution, my principles will be undermined. I will no longer be my own man. I will not be allowed to speak truth to power…that is my responsibility as a Chicano intellectual. You compromise that obligation by taking on the role of serving the state and the institution. It's bullshit that young people have to go to school to conform versus having the chance to be themselves. I always tell a young scholar to never compromise who you are. You have to compromise some of this to survive, but, never let the institution force you to compromise for the sake of getting ahead.

Words like "be your own man," "compromise," "principles," are key constructs that define David's ideological standpoint as a certain type of Chicano scholarship boy. Like the scholarship boy, Carlos (discussed later in this chapter), the act of *servin'* serves a metaphor for: reshaping, reimaging, controlling. Knowledge is something *to get* and it is used in a way that provides independence of thought and action. It also fulfills the "manly" struggle to *make things fair* for the self and the larger oppressed community of people of color.

How many working-class Latino men in the United States are able to address masculinity intellectually and feel fulfilled? The statistics point to a severe high school drop-out/push-out emergency and working-class communities are often void of resources that allow young men to pursue knowledge in a way such as David. That is what makes David's journey in part, very remarkable. Very much, a "ghetto nerd" (Diaz, 2007), in a "cool" way I must say, he speaks to the ways *manhood yearning* can be expressed in a mentally challenging way. Negative masculinity and its often-violent appendage of violent machismo, can be mediated with immersion within intellectual, critical, and spiritual self-analysis. The elements of competition, independence, respect, honor, and struggle for individual autonomy can work within a gendering process that sees the intersectionality of race, class, and gender as reference points of valuable knowledge which can help in solidifying one's *place at the table.* As Valenzuela (1999) points out, nonetheless, schooling for Latin@s living in the United States often translates to a subtractive process of continuous disfranchisement. So, for working-class Mexican-origin males, "doing gender" in a way that furthers academic excellence is rare and quite difficult. In the U.S. and many other parts of the world, "being a boy" is increasingly correlated with academic underachievement. This has been an escalating problem. Research on boys in schools (Epstein, Elwood, Hey, & Maw, 1998; Mac & Ghaill, 1994; Saenz & Ponjuan, 2009) points to the polemic term, but nonetheless, useful idea of an emerging "crisis" to describe the education/schooling outcomes of boys in England, Australia, and the United States.

Antonio: I Don't Need College to Answer My Own Questions

Antonio, the scholarship boy with a consistent existential angst, often made mention about how knowledge was "his" and created "by him." Like the other scholarship boys in this study, he uses "brains" as the most masculine source of strength. His standpoint entails that he views "his" brains as having something so organic and critical that he can out-compete (at the level of debate, knowledge possession, and nuanced philosophical oratory) any economically privileged Latin@ or White students.

> *I'm from the barrio, so therefore, I know how to make something out of nothing. While the schools think they are putting me in my place, as a brown boy from the ghetto, I actually put them in their place. I don't have disadvantage, I put people in check intellectually – like a rapper, a good one. I realized that outside of school and in school, as a little boy, that Mexicans, like me, have to teach themselves. Shit, you think Dr. Seuss can teach me about my world?*

Outside of his own search for meaning, he gave very little credit to his K-12 teachers or his undergraduate and graduate education. In fact, the race, class, and gender norms of middle class, Whitestream universities (and K-12 schools) haunt him to this day. He elaborates:

> *In elementary school you learn about white heroes. In college you learn that you are kind of a human, but you are not "the human." So, I can't*

> *tell you that professors and teachers ever knew what it means to be me. It was about being colonized into white magic, ideas, and that is why I do have a posttraumatic story. The barrio, its between me and some doctor and God. When I told teachers about how Mexicans are screwed over by society, they always responded in school: "why do you have to be so negative?"*

Antonio, who is now in his early forties, rejects the idea of White people serving him information that is valuable. He rejects the notion that assimilation is good and that he, as a "poor" Latino boy should be thankful for the fruits of his labor and schooling. Over the course of our talks, all he kept saying was: *I teach myself and whenever a white boy at the gym or in school said something stupid, I had to tell them the facts.* David believes that he owns "the facts" and he is happy, willing, and able to continuously put up "his facts" against teachers, students, and every day folk who claim that the United States is some type of panacea of hope and a fair playing field. It is also connects to common theme in the working-class life of many Latino boys who live in urban communities related to the gendering norms of: "authenticity," "respect," "holding your ground," and "defending oneself from attacks."

"Brown" masculinities consistently in relational interactions with often violent norms in school. For Antonio, he recalls, in a very Freirian (1971) sense, refusing to become an object of production. He recalls always pursuing his historical subjectivity even if it means not meeting linear notions of success. Latino manhood is shaped by his constant debate with schooling expectations and knowledge claims. He explains:

> *You know, it's painful. I went to school, dreaming that something there was good for me. So, I go from the abuse of poverty and gang fights in my block to high school, which was basically a McDonalds, we (Latinos) are the fast food of human beings. Nobody cared about us in high school, we were their paychecks. So, I dropped out of high school. No fear, I dropped out and got a GED. I went to my local library and bookshelf; I read everything I could get my hands on. School was useless, they didn't teach me anything. In less than two days, I passed the GED, it was a breeze, super easy.*

This "dropping out" phase was an exercise of power against system oppression. Unlike much of the literature (e.g.,Willis, 1977) that suggests that many males drop out or develop counter-school attitudes, in part, because of macho cultures that socialize them into thinking school is "gay" or "too feminine" (part of the discourse of what is referred to as a "masculinity crisis"); for Antonio, school in its institutional sense, was a rejection of him (raced, classed, and gendered self), not the other way around. He loves the "idea" of school and learning. To this day, he only sleeps about 3 hours a day. He spends most of time reading the world and the word (Freire, 1970). His scholarship boy journey encompasses intense feelings of rejection and the search for autonomy in very cyclical ways. School became a place where he his manhood is questioned in its ontological, historical, political, and sociocultural dimensions. Antonio takes this as a challenge, one he is always ready to struggle against. It is his love for learning that did push him to go back to school over and over, until earning his graduate degree (in spite of the microagressions). In fact as he puts it, *school is where I went to war and tested myself, that is where I found out where I stood, so I did go to school with the intention of doing well. I was not down with the idea of being a ruthless guy hanging out on the street and being dumb as hell.*

Like Willis's (1977) study of the *lad's* (set in a British schooling context), Antonio demonstrates a rejection of his masculine self being turned into something else—in his case, as he puts it: *a white boy.* The difference is of course, that Antonio uses strategic counterstances to continue his education and pursue social class mobility while at the same time rejecting certain hegemonic forces germane to schooling. David has internalized an oppositional, yet dialectical identity with the forces of cultural domination. Similar to Ferguson's (2001) ethnographic of African American boys in an urban high school, Antonio is constantly feeling like his masculinity (with its raced and classed intersections) puts him a conundrum: perform the cues of the dominant culture or else pay the consequences of being considered a "bad boy." For Antonio, there is a prolonged and difficult burden of performing whiteness all while contesting its very centeredness. Antonio elaborates:

> *Right away I knew I belonged to the "bad group." The poor Mexicans. They looked at us like that, teachers and society. As a kid, I just looked around, and I was like, shit! We, Chicanos are broke! But why? So I went to school, wanting to find out why. But, I just had to sit there, with the teachers telling me to follow all these rules. I know they probably thought all Mexicans would just keep quiet, I didn't, I talked back and* made *my points. In high school, the vatos were doing crazy stuff, so then, I was having to work with that stigma, of being just another vato causing trouble. You know, I get dizzy just thinking about of all the different battles.*

Antonio, in his constant push for naming his location and in metaphorical terms, eliciting a subpoena against intellectual and cultural genocide, often spins into a surreal, hyper-poetic stream of consciousness. This incoherence, madness, and genius are tainted with doses of disappointment and prolonged yearning. Like Rodriguez (1982), his "hunger of memory" almost has him frozen in time. He says: *what happened to that boy, the one with candy, near the tree house? Am I the man I could have been?*

Antonio's gendered life course is in part about not adhering to a careful, timid, and externally controlled life course. He wants to be in control. Due to a spinal injury as kid, Antonio gets certain economic benefits that he counts as his only source of income at this present moment. He has not cashed in on his education. Antonio says:

> *These 29,000 dollar a year jobs, that's all I was offered. Those broke jobs. If I was a white boy, I'd be the director of a major motion picture company by now. Doors open up for them in ways a book will never be able to explain, it's the racism of the system. It has always been that way.*

Antonio spends his days reading, making his own movies at home, and dreaming about a *better place.* He made it clear to me that he will not struggle within a system that pays out different benefits based on race, class, and gender. He instead, prefers to live on his own terms, learning at his own pace and seeing how he can make his dream of owning a film studio come true. There is also a certain kind of "racial battle fatigue" (Smith et al., 2006) and conscientization that he has gone through since earning his masters degree. Antonio appears to be less willing now, in his forties, to insert himself within hegemonic structures of any form. Since he feels like he has the "facts" (or can get them on his own), his goal is now to put them into practical use. Moreover, unlike Paz's (1985) view that suffering is a central culprit for the masks that Mexicans wear, Antonio pursues his sociocultural, race, class, and gendered self with much more clarity now due to the information he got from the pain he suffered germane to his ongoing scholarship boy journey.

Mario: I Do Not Sleep with the Devil in That Way

Mario used the term "devil" to describe mainstream ideas and goals/rituals. As he puts it: *I make a conscious effort not to move with the norm. If the logic is not right, then it's not right.* Moving between an intense sensitivity and anger, Mario forged a very poetic, almost romantic-utopian view about how life should be lived. He elaborates:

I know that the norm is unjust in historical terms and has been oppressive to Latinos, and does not relate to us. We can attach ourselves to it. We do it unconsciously sometimes, we follow the flow, but, I catch it, I see when I go into the sell out category. Moving up is defined by whom? Knowledge is defined by whom? The dominant culture defines it. You don't move up until they give you credentials and you follow their rules.

Mario grew up in working-class community where he remembers most of his friends dropping out of school. He remembers a certain working-class intimacy and solidarity with their struggles, and finds academia and Eurocentric norms as "stealing" something about his core essence. From K-8th grade, he was an honor student. In high school, teachers played the role of security guards and punishers. He recalls:

I was in high school, pretty much like a Marxist. I had studied Fidel Castro, Cesar Chavez, and Saul Alinsky. The machine, the white, middle class machine of production; I knew it was about stealing and looting. I would challenge teachers on their blind spots. But they didn't want to hear it, I even got suspended because of it.

High school was a time of negotiations with the way brown, Latino boys were seen framed by campus administrators and many teachers: dumb, violent, and out of control. Mario was not labeled as a promising student anymore. Suddenly, teachers viewed him as a threat and as another hypermasculine barrio boy that was not particularly interested in school.

The use of the words "norm" and "mainstream" were in constant use as he told me about his survival/coping strategies. For Mario, schooling hides silences, and indoctrinates with false notions of common sense. This is the violence he says he constantly, *catches*. Imagine him as a lifelong ethnographer, using critical literacy to debunk myths. Unlike the academically successful *schoolboys* in Ferguson's (2001) excellent study of African American masculinity in an urban high school, doing gender for Mario encompasses not hiding his working-class aesthetic to get ahead and do well in school.

Like the other scholarship boys in this study, Mario is an avid reader. He uses "brains" instead of fists in his "fights." He defended himself from hegemonic schooling norms not by getting poor grades or dropping out of school but by reading more, so he could debate against the threats (ideology of schools' hidden and overt curriculum, teacher standpoints) in more eloquent ways. His mind is his weapon; it is his source of ultimate power. When the system comes at him one way, he outmaneuvers it with school smarts/street smarts. He is a barrio boy and "nerd," and uses a switch-hitting approach to sociocultural violence. He believes that the system is setup to destroy the Latino male. He perceives schooling structures as systems that continuously tracks Latino males from urban schools into working-class jobs. Even for the "successful" Latino students like him, he still believes that he is being setup to lose his "authentic" barrio boy identity if he follows all of the rituals of middle class public life and schooling. There is not the epic, rising up or "making it" it feeling. Instead, the irony is that "making it" has a racialized, classed, and gendered soul – a subtractive prize that he begins to question over time.

Mario loves the idea of learning and going to school. But, he has a counter school attitude as it relates the way schooling produces the educated man. Unlike the lads in Willis's (1977) research on working-class males, Mario's counter schooling ideology is not a linear rejection of its academic expectations. He does not wholeheartedly reject the steps, rituals, and performances necessary to do well in school. He is a doctoral student at a top tier university. Instead, he performs battles with professors, peers, and even himself as he continuously disrupts the social constructions of "natural flow" of things all while not completely being "kicked out" of the system. He rebels by taking time off from school without giving any explanations or he goes into deeply melancholic states where he goes through an intense existential angst. He explains:

> *I am not about top down, I am about relationships. I am about love. Top down people make it all neatly, right through the system. That includes most whites and 'Hispanics' from the middle class. They call those people, the 'grown ups.' Fuck that, I am about knowing knowledge and people in deep ways, leading with the critical use of the mind. In school, we have constant competition, with winners, losers, and sell-outs. We have no middle ground. I hate that. It kills me and the youth, it is so masculine in that way.*

On more than one occasion, Mario cried when talking about these issues. He says, *I am hard on the outside, but my emotional, sensitive inside, is what makes me so smart and aware. That's why I don't fall for the hype of just being a student the way they want me to be, there is something more to life.* I must admit that when I heard him say this, I got a little emotional.

A stunning literature gap remains in the masculinity research, where it fails to account for how being "hard" and resisting school norms, is not necessarily representative of having a hypermasculine, macho attitude in its entirety. Instead, as in the case of Mario, we see how much he suffers and how sensitive he really is. He is thoughtful, reflective, and deeply in touch with the social and dialectical dimension of identity creation. He uses this pain, one full of memories of oppression in historical terms as it relates to Chicana@s and Mexicans, to fight back in public, but then goes home into a recluse of reflection. He refuses to let the *devil* (dominant culture – using his language) go uncontested.

His struggle with the *devil* is increasingly difficult now that he is trying to write his dissertation:

> *When I write, I feel like I lose some of my manhood as I feel it. I am raw, I want to write from the subconscious, to tell my story as I experienced it. But, what does the university expect? A soft, white, in the box, super organized paper. The battle is: will I become a system writer? If I fall into the trap, I have just allowed my experience to be destroyed and ignored. Every word I write is a crisis for me. It's a struggle of life and death. Too them, the professors, I am a whiner, to me, it's about keeping my life. I have no desire to be a coconut.*

The crisis of masculinity is vested in part within how Mario sees the university as possessing a white, middle class/elite masculinity. This view of masculinity consists of the idea that higher education embodies a certain raced, gendered, and classed standpoint that informs its formal and hidden curriculum. He continuously "acts up" and battles against it by disappearing from the system and sometimes by using his "brains" to strategize on how he can have his way. He says:

> *I put people in check in my classes, you know the assimilated ones. I have to give them the information they forgot to learn at Harvard. Their egos are all up there, but whether it's the professor or most of the students, I found out they couldn't catch me intellectually. They are all somehow involved in this twisted colonizing machine. I caught it, and trust me I let them know about it.*

Mario, then, constructs the self, in part, through intellectual fight stories. *La lucha* (the struggle), to save face, is one that he is likely going to the grave with. Unlike gangs that engage in brown on brown crime, Mario contends that *devil* usually does not look like him or have his positionality. The norms of the hegemonic knowledge structure and its values enrage him. He also views the dominant culture as being full of pathological layers, tainted by a long history of absolute notions of success, education, and morality which are morally and intellectually bankrupt. He explains:

> *I know that the norm is unjust in historical terms and has been oppressive to Latinos, and does not relate to us. We can attach ourselves to it. We do it unconsciously sometimes, we follow the flow, but, I catch it, I see when I go into the sell out category. Moving up is defined by whom? Knowledge is defined by whom? The dominant culture defines it, you don't move up until they give you credentials and you follow their rules.*

Thinking of this statement makes me reflect on how Mario came to be involved in this project. He read the essay I wrote, *Lost in Degree: A Chicano PhD student's Search for Missing Clothes* (2007), and emailed me. He said, *that's me, I know that pain.* Being a barrio boy, a scholarship boy at that, took him into spaces few of his peers ever went. But, he merges that distance by competing, controlling, and resisting much of the ontological and epistemological notions of becoming educated in any normative sense. The barrio, never really has left him. Without it, he could never really call himself, a well-educated Latino man of letters.

Carlos: I Loved Servin' Them

As mentioned in the introduction, I connected with Carlos's metaphor of *servin'*. Growing up in barrio communities in Los Angeles, I often engaged in a discourse of "proving oneself" while embodying a certain air of confidence ingrained in the body-politics of urban, working-class ontology. For Carlos, letting people know that they had to earn their voice of legitimacy is important. He elaborates: *Fools think because of their pedigree that I'm supposed to respect them. A lot of the people I served though, I ultimately did end up having love for.* Carlos conducted some type of sociocultural and intellectual audit on his graduate school peers. When knowledge claims were not up to his standard, he called them out on it and *served them* with the information he deemed accurate, critical, and more nuanced.

For Carlos, *servin'* has a long history. While his recollections of elementary school are quite positive (he cherished the intimacy and caring from teachers), middle school through high school consisted mostly of psychological, cultural, and emotional microaggressions. In elementary school, he was framed as intelligent, but, now things changed.

> *You were full of potential then (elementary school). I had two teachers the whole year in one class. In middle school you had so much change from class to class. The family feel was gone.*

Potential is framed as the way the teacher-institutional gaze looked at him. Carlos remembers feeling protected in elementary school and being perceived as smart. From middle school to high school, he says: *it was my body, you know, it didn't look like the body of the "smart kids."* Carlos walks with a certain Chicano swagger, his clothes appear to not be purchased at any middle class outlet or shopping mall. He has some of the Chicano posture common in many urban spaces. His boyhood to adolescence transition was now perceived a threat. Like in the case of the "troublemakers" in Ferguson's study (2001) on African American masculinity, he could sense that officially sanctioned paths to academic success were now blocked to him. This was a stunning and anger filled assessment. Whereas before middle school he was happy to work in dialectical terms with teachers, now it was about *servin'* hegemonic forces. He says:

> *Teachers you know, if they disrespected me, I spoke up. I turned it off and on (academically) as I pleased. An example is 10th grade, I took this test (end of year standardized test) and I got all of the questions right. I got put in AP History but I got out of it.*

Similar to the scholarship boy Mario, he turned off his ability to perform well academically when he felt that he was being disrespected or when teachers didn't *bring it* (did not give him quality, critical, rigorous schooling/ education). Carlos ends up connecting his mind and body (and soul) and seeks to speak, reject, and contest schooling on his terms. This is usually a death sentence for most urban, barrio youth. But, what keeps Carlos "thinking" and intellectually (and spiritually) satisfied is his dedication to reading. This is a trait exemplified by all the scholarship boys in this research. He explains:

> *The library was a sanctuary. A place to workout. A workshed of mind. I was a four or five times a day type of library person. I would get one or two books and read quick and go back. At the library I could remember that I was intelligent. Reading there reminded me that intense intelligence. I would just sit on the isle. I would also go to 7-Eleven (store) at age 9 and 10 and get magazine subscriptions so I can order material to read.*

So unlike the work of Willis (1977) on working-class masculinity and counter-school identities, Carlos gains “power” and “manhood honor” by putting in academic labor and from his control, mastery, and interactions with independent inquiry and his strategic use of “brains.” His ability and confidence in serving people comes from his independent search for knowledge and meaning. Also, there is nuanced take on being “hard.” Being a complete, strong “man,” means standing your ground, defending yourself, mainly through the means of intellect. Masculinity is an intellectual performance that requires a lot of isolation and self-teaching. The library and books are what gives him power to fight back. It many ways, Carlos sees his intellect as something that requires intense exercise, for the purpose pursuing social justice ends and also for protection of the brown body and psyche against the larger, racialized, classed, and gender social structures that do not norm people “like him” as worthy of “success” and “smartness.”

Research on masculinities is clear about men wanting respect and recognition. How boys/men act out this request is crucial. There is not a particularly neat story about Carlos’s approach. Carlos left high school for a few months and did not attend college until after a few years after high school. He did not take a privileged, hyper-protected journey towards earning a doctorate in human development at one of the most prestigious research one universities in the nation. Instead, he learned how to work with ambivalence. Like Hoggart’s (1957) description of the scholarship boy, Carlos was never a full member of any group. This type of psychological distance helps in the reflexive sense. *Servin’* is part of what Richard Rodriguez did in *Hunger of Memory* (1982). He rejected certain tropes of identity politics. As mentioned previously, a central dimension of the survival instinct of scholarship boys is: *the construction of self through intellectual fight stories*. Rodriguez does it. And so does everyone in this study.

Servin’ is a struggle, a fight, a dual, a positioning of ontology, epistemology, and history. Its inspiration is partly inspired by a miseducation. Carlos explains:

> *Not until my first year of community college did my historical self come up. The rest was like a vacation from who you are. The one thing that was right there, Carlos, was never covered until community college.*

Searching for the complex sociocultural self was solely an independent project until community college. His struggle still did not end though, as he worked to *serve* certain students and instructors. Carlos’s gendered life course is consistently interacting with how he performs his brains in a schooling context, to defend himself, or teach someone about what they are "missing." Carlos is a man of reason, but not one that believes that the private and public require separation (i.e. unlike Richard Rodriguez). His standpoint stems from the hybridity of consciousness, drawing largely from how barrio and formal schooling demands interact. He positions his mind as the deciding factor (driven largely by memory, synthesis, spirituality, and "knowledge").

The Latino masculinities of working-class youth are often part of a "dominated aesthetic" (Bourdieu, 1984). Carlos points to the way manhood in a brown, working-class body and context can move towards emancipation from the hegemonic gaze. Intellectual defiance against the oppressor requires a tenacity of self education and occasional performance that may seem "erratic." He explains:

> *It was crazy there (at his undergraduate university). I just wanted more truth there. Got some bullshit work. I got a few bad grades here and there. Sometimes I didn't even go…I just can't pull of the whole just go with the flow thing. I have to be comfortable with myself.*

There is this certain kind of resistance against just going with the flow while still acknowledging that school matters. Carlos said that the always saw himself as a professor. His journey illustrates the messy, ambivalent, and difficult path for many Latino males.

Schools have certain spaces and teachers that can help in a positive way. Nonetheless, taking into consideration the common marginalization and deficit views toward Latino males in U.S. urban schools, Carlos demonstrates that the hardness and rage of a poverty stricken, urban upbringing, can be channeled into an ambitious intellectual work ethic. In this way, one can *serve* the system and their definitions of knowledge, self, and success. It is not easy and it has its on markers and scars.

SUMMARY

> Whiteness and maleness and middle-classness intersect in a form of embodiment that populates certain social spaces with a living norm of ontological power. (Perkinson, 2002, p. 175)

Working-class masculinities in schools are often correlated with low educational outcomes. The case of scholarship boys demonstrates a different correlation. This chapter illustrates how Mexican-origin scholarship boys can resist many school cultural norms and still do well academically. Doing "well" is not a clean, linear, and coherent process. There are ups and downs. Thus, there is not a linear success pattern for all students, but instead cyclical entry and exit points where some scholarship boys may be outside of the statistics of academic excellence at varying junctures. One of the scholarship boys (Carlos) dropped out of high school for a few months and realized, *hard labor is not for me.* Unlike the *lads* in Willis's (1977) study of working-class males in a British secondary school, "pen-pushing" is considered a legitimate masculine thing to do for scholarship boys (p. 96). Cultivating the brain carries a masculine ethos. With information, you can fight back and define yourself, on your terms (at least in part). Mario elicits a continuous rebellion. But he centers this process as "normal." The scholarship boys "serve" the dominant class with their ideas on what it mean to be *educated.* They refuse to take in knowledge as is. They work to control the discourse of becoming an educated Latino male all while being cognizant of the cultural capital expectations for brown bodies in Eurocentric schools. The problematic dimensions of expecting academic success in linear systems of schooling for working-class Latino males that have non-linear lives is part of the set-up for creating academic achievement gaps. Whereas many working-class youth internalize the socialization dimensions of being called or framed as "dumb," the scholarship boys (regardless of occasional academic ups and downs) in this research believed since childhood that they are *really smart.* They "do gender" by controlling their minds in intense ways that help in resisting deficit views. They *hit the books* with the rigor of a really good street fighter.

In a very scholarship boy fashion, "success" is envisioned as a discourse which is part of a social construction that emasculates scholarships boys in certain racialized and classed ways. *Their* (dominant class) success is not success. Achievement slogans like "making it" are forced to consider the thoughts of Latino males from the barrio. This chapter demonstrates that the transformation in class consciousness through a racial intersection informs much of the resistance of Mexican-origin scholarship boys. All of the scholarship boys in this study have a critical understanding of Chican@ history and their sociohistorical subjectivity. They also came of age in the colonial and decolonial alyers of living in Aztlán. Their critical awareness and ideas around power were shaped largely by their intense affinity for reading since they were children and due to their nuanced reflections across time germane to being Latino, male, and poor, in urban America. Interestingly, none of the scholarship boys spoke of family members who were also into reading with the same type of fervor. Unlike Rodriguez (1982), who attended middle class K-12 schools, the subjects in this study attended low SES, urban public schools. Their socialization encompassed developing distaste for "selling out." Not selling out and talking back to hegemony is at the core of what it means to reach authentic, scholarly manhood. Some of these codes of authenticity, honor, self-respect, and integrity, are part of the linguistic and ideological discourses of barrio life. Keeping it real and calling out posers, wanna-be's, fakes, *cococunuts*, are a normal part of daily transactions of solidarity. The excellence in their intellectual repertoire is based on a clever psycho-spiritual dance, where they move between multiple worlds.

In light of banking schooling models and neoliberal, market driven approaches to schooling that are all the rave in the United States, scholarship boys are positioned as insider-outsider students of excellence. In the masculine halls of school, where one must engage in battle for academic supremacy, scholarship boys do compete, and usually fair quite well. But, as in the case of Mario, winning all the time is not really a good thing. He claims to sometimes "fail" on purpose: *sometimes I sabotage opportunities, on purpose; to make sure I keep my soul. I know I will still get what I want in the end.* The compromises that scholarship boys have to make for academic supremacy are thus analyzed with a very spiritual, sociocultural, and ethical stance. Sometimes, as in David's case, he has to *keep it real* and see what happens (proven by his stance on publishing, he refused to join the publish or perish mantra – and still was able to get tenure). Moreover, affinity for the needs of their working-class community, social justice, and critical reorganization of schools and knowledge is very much part of their standpoint.

Most of the scholarship on masculinties examines the lives of White males. Much of this work comes from research conducted in England and Australia. Generally, intersections with race and ethnicity in urban, inner city schools (in the U.S.) receive a very uncritical and passive analysis. Rios's (2011) ethnography of Black and Latino boys in Oakland, California, is one critical take on the hypercriminalization of these young men. The work presented in this chapter aims at contributing to this gap. The scholarship boys in this chapter demonstrate how Latino working-class males can seek a sense of cultural autonomy while pursing schooling in a largely subtractive context. You do not have to necessarily use fists to fight back. The use of "brains" is crucial for it provides a salient leverage point by which to develop power and recognition. The library may be the best ally a barrio boy can have. Not the teacher, but the library. The allies are the authors and critical thinkers that may give voice to one's story and emancipation. The author's words become part of an imaginary world. They inhabited a world of thinkers and philosophers and generally, they don't tend to reject you, block you, or restrict you from your path. Books don't usually call you dumb or loser (although I am conscious of books that do just that). Books do not give you a standardized test. The power of self-teaching and relating it to reading the world (Freire & Macedo, 1987), is what in essence, frees a Mexican-origin scholarship boy from some doses of second class, colonial citizenship and self destructive hypermasculinity. Malcolm X, a certain type of scholarship boy, exemplifies the point. After being told by his teacher that he should work with his hands because he was black and thus should be "realistic" in his aims to become a lawyer, his life spun out of control. Reading (of course, some of this reading entailed the strong devotion he developed for the Nation of Islam) during his jail sentence connected him with a sense of liberation and agency, which took him through a unique path of discovery and greatness. Male blackness meant something different once he got to teach himself.

Drawing from the work of Farrell (1974), liberated men must *flow* to avoid "emotional constipation" (p. 71). For Mexican-origin scholarship boys, *servin'* is a release, a satisfying letting go and letting out. This liberates them from hyper-commitment to traditional gender roles that fail to examine how patriarchy injures them. The story of the Mexican-origin scholarship boy is one of vulnerable confession. This release centers their social justice philosophy and cultivates their emotional approach to holistic growth as Latino men of letters.

CHAPTER 5

TOWARD A GHETTO NERD FRAMEWORK[1]

> Theorists-of-color are in the process of trying to formulate "marginal" theories that are partially outside and partially inside the Western frame of reference (if that is possible), theories that overlap many "worlds."
> (Gloria Anzaldúa, 1990)

> No le tengas miedo a los gringos. Tu sabes mas que todos ellos. (Don't be afraid of white people. You know more than all of them.)
> (Celida Angulo Carrillo, author's mother)

It was a cold and grey January day in Cambridge, Massachusetts.[2] I entered the Harvard University campus (where I was attending a lecture by Howard Gardner) and I was suddenly reminded of the surreal journey that had brought me to this point. As a high school student, I had been told, and reminded, by my teachers that nobody from my barrio would ever write a book. During my junior year of high school, a Los Angeles Police Department officer pulled me over while crossing the street on a busy Los Angeles boulevard and, at gun point, told me that one day I would grow up to be a drug addict and dealer. I had swallowed a burn and rage for much of life. I was fortunate that my mother provided me with advice that nurtured my resistance to arguments around my intellectual inferiority and hyper-criminalization. Unfortunately, there are many working-class, Latin@[3] intellectual and cultural border-crossers, who are marginalized by current definitions of achievement, cultural notions of intelligence, and deficit discourses germane to the Latin@ community. Moreover, psychometrics, a field of study that focuses on the measurement of human abilities, often dismisses us because it *can't see us* in our full complexity. Historically, this approach to measurement has led to the conception of the Intelligence Quotient (IQ), and has been highly influential in the development of school assessments, which ultimately have been used to label minority students as not particularly intelligent—or not as intelligent as Whites (Suzuki & Valencia, 1997; Valdés, 2003; Valencia, 2002). Kincheloe (2004) makes a similar critique when arguing that the unintelligent tend to be framed as, "…those people, who in terms of culture, race, sexual orientation, gender, or economic status, are different from the psychologists creating the classification system" (p. 15).

For working-class, Mexican-origin males, many of them interact with what Rios (2011) refers to as the *youth control complex*, a systemic apparatus of oppression and criminalization that comes from the way their identities are conceptualized by entities such as the police, the media, businesses, and schools. Furthermore, an apparatus governed by the discipline of psychology, attempts to de-intellectualize Latin@ students while simultaneously centering the common sense of dominant notions of how intelligence and success must be demonstrated and embodied. Notions of who gets to theorize and how intelligence is allowed to be performed are deeply imbedded in our social system and are profoundly hegemonic. In other words, it is the enactment of very specific behaviors, discourses, and styles, usually characteristics of white, middle-class dispositions, that are associated with being intelligent. As such, being male, of Mexican descent, working-class, and being viewed as academically "successful" is, in many respects, rare. Historically, working-class Latino male bodies have not been associated with intelligence. In fact, there is nearly a double percentage gap of white male students enrolled in gifted and talented programs compared to Latino males (Torres & Fergus, 2011), only 49% of Latino males graduate from high school in the U.S. (Greene & Winters, 2006), and Latino males are overrepresented in low-wage labor (Noguera, Hurtado, & Fergus, 2012).

Dominant notions of intelligence and "common-sense" ideas of the social positions in which working-class Latinos belong have continued the cycle of theoretical frameworks that fail to recognize and analyze the intelligences, knowledge, and sophisticated skills developed by those successfully straddling subjugated and hegemonic cultural worlds. It is, thus, not surprising that very few studies have explored the identities and trajectories of high-achieving Mexican-origin males as scientifically valid sources to potentially inform conceptions of intelligence and giftedness.

This chapter focuses on Mexican-origin heterosexual male students that were born and raised in low-income urban settings. To explore their culturally situated intelligences, I introduce the *Mestiz@*[4] *Theory of Intelligences* (MTI). This theory emphasizes the talents, improvisations, and intelligences used by some working-class Mexican-origin students in an effort to excel academically, spiritually, and culturally. Moreover, this work introduces *critical mestizaje* (CM) as a form of intelligence whereby the cultural production of intelligence(s) centers the narratives and abilities that draw from the intersections of race, class, gender, and the migratory consciousness of the oppressed. Specifically, I use "critical mestizaje" (Pérez-Torres, 2006) as one of the key theories that informs MTI. Pérez-Torres explains CM below:

> Mestizaje embodies the idea of multiple subjectivities, opening up discussion of identity to greater complexity and nuance. Critical mestizaje locates how people live their lives in and through their bodies as well as in and through ideology. (p. xiii)

This critical form of mestizaje better accounts for the border-crossing intelligences of working-class students such as the Mexican-origin scholarship boys in this research. Moreover, this definition captures how liminal identities interact with various forms of domination. This research focuses on Multiple Intelligences (MI) theory as a reference point because it has had a significant impact on the intelligences debate. Further, it provides fertile ground for exploration, as it fails to account for certain intelligences that may come from living in the margins.

The work herein seeks to contribute to this research gap by utilizing MTI and providing examples of how some working-class students demonstrate "intelligence."

SUBTRACTIVE SCHOOLING AND UNACKNOWLEDGED INTELLIGENCES

Growing up on welfare in south Los Angeles, California barrios immersed me in what are considered *subtractive schooling* (Valenzuela, 1999) contexts. Furthermore, I experienced the 1992 Los Angeles uprising, racial profiling by police, a series of migratory experiences between Mexico, the U.S., and various linguistic and sociocultural contexts. Living a life through and in-between different cultures, languages, and social groups with often conflicting values, and expectations became commonplace. My life was about survival, it was about cultural literacies, it was about equity and justice, and it was about being "at least twice as gifted" (Carrillo, 2010). I navigated multiple worlds and developed complex identities that addressed the needs of each. I never felt like I was "slow." That is, I never saw myself as remedial. What I came to find out, nonetheless, was that I did not exist alone. I was positioned (in the U.S.) as part of group that was not "smart enough" for traditional measurements. The social contract I was born into largely failed to account for the psychic, spiritual, cultural, and physical crossing of intellectual and cultural borders that often is a core piece of the identities of working-class Latin@ students. Many working-class Latino males are intellectual breakdancers[5] who negotiate much more than bubbling in the correct answer on a test. In other words, they maneuver through multiple settings, ideologies, and identities.

MI: MEETING GARDNER AND UNPACKING THE THEORY

In 2008, I was a Spencer dissertation fellow while pursuing a doctorate at the University of Texas at Austin. The Spencer Foundation provided me with the opportunity to have a discussion with Howard Gardner.[6] I was interested in hearing how his views related to my thinking. While I was thankful for the time he gave me as an overzealous graduate student, I do not think I made much headway with my explanation about how intelligence may look when attending to subaltern communities. In my conversation with Gardner, I tried to hint at the fact that I examine "different" intelligences in ways that are not adequately captured by his framework. Minorities in the U.S. have long been framed as the non-intelligent sector of our population (Kincheloe & Steinberg, 1997). There are deficit undercurrents in No Child Left Behind, and there exists a long history of using singular units like IQ scores for claiming particular gifts that, for some reason, students of color do not seem to "have" in significant numbers. Additionally, teachers often use student performances of "smartness" to identify gifted pupils (Hatt, 2007; Suzuki & Valencia, 1997; Valdés, 2003). These teacher identifications are often based on the ability of a student to perform certain forms of middle class *cultural capital.*[7] Also, even under the theory of *Multiple Intelligences* (Gardner, 1985), there is little that addresses the terms of how working-class Latino students are "intellectually imagined." Hatt (2007) explains a relevant point:

> …the ways smartness is constructed within schools is especially harmful for racially, ethnically, and economically marginalized youth. Smartness operates as a powerful factor in the education of marginalized students who are often wrongfully left feeling or labeled as incompetent or 'slow.' (p. 149)

MI theory is an important contribution and an extension of previous thinking on intelligences. Gardner challenges the usefulness and validity of a single measure of intelligence (IQ scores). However, his theory remains bounded by the strengths and limitations of Western thought, Cartesian rationality, psychological scholarship, and claims of objectivity. As Kincheloe (2004) points out, MI theory is also: "antidemocratic, supportive of an abstract individualism, epistemologically naïve, subversive of community, insensitive to race and socioeconomic class issues, patriarchal, Western colonialist, Eurocentric" (p. 7).

According to Gardner, there are eight core intelligences: bodily-kinesthetic, interpersonal, linguistic, logical-mathematical, naturalistic, intrapersonal, spatial, and musical. Bodily-kinesthetic pertains to the ability to skillfully use one's body to achieve particular goals. Dancers, basketball players, and tennis players are among those who display this type of intelligence. Interpersonal reflects one's ability to understand (and perceive) other peoples' emotions, feelings, moods, etc. Politicians, parents, and teachers often fit into this category. Linguistic intelligence concerns the ability to use language to achieve particular goals, sensitivity to language (both spoken and written), and the ability to learn multiple languages. Gardner (2006) cites T.S. Eliot's ability to create the magazine *Fireside* (at age 10) and publish eight complete issues in a three-day period as example of someone having this intelligence (p. 13). Logical-mathematical intelligence consists of gifted abilities in terms of problem solving and working with logical systems. Gardner (2006) contends that this intelligence "…has been thoroughly investigated by traditional psychologists…" (p. 12). He also cites a long, documented history of the existence of this type of intelligence in children as a result of the work of Piaget (Gardner, 2006, p. 12). Naturalistic intelligence refers to sensitivity to plants, animals, and other aspects of the natural world, including clouds and various topographical formations. Gardner suggests that this is an intelligence used by farmers and even by consumers when buying items such as shoes and clothes. Those with intrapersonal intelligence have a strong sensitivity and understanding of one's own emotions. Counselors and motivational speakers may possess this form of intelligence. Spatial intelligence emphasizes the ability to think in three dimensions. Among the capacities that make up this intelligence are spatial reasoning, mental imagery, image manipulation, and active imagination. Musical intelligence focuses on the ability to discern and create music. Key elements are also the abilities to reflect on, discern, and reproduce music. Composers and vocalists are among those that have this intelligence.

In sum, Gardner's MI theory, an example of a dominant discourse surrounding intelligence, provides a crucial step towards expanding our views on how intelligence looks and is performed by various individuals. Nonetheless, MI Theory's limitations leave ample room for reconceptualizing intelligences in more nuanced, contextual, critical, and inclusive ways. The theory remains decontextualized and not critical of various issues germane to, but not limited to, race, gender, power, class, and history. Given this, the goal of MTI is to build on and extend MI theory by taking into account the particularities of marginalized communities and individuals.

TOWARDS A MESTIZ@ THEORY OF INTELLIGENCES (MTI)

This work looks at critical mestizaje and how it is utilized by scholarship boys in ways that demonstrate intelligences that are different from those in Gardner's MI framework. Additionally, Anzaldúa's (1987) mestiza consciousness informed my conceptualization of the Mestiz@ Theory of Intelligences. According to Anzaldúa (1987), a mestiza consciousness is a form of critical consciousness that embodies the complexities, tensions, ambiguities, contradictions, and history of the U.S.-Mexican borderlands. This lens is useful for understanding how various border-crossers, such as scholarship boys, negotiate hybridity and the contradictions inherent to various sites of cultural and social difference. I do not claim that the scholarship boys in this chapter embody a mestiza consciousness, for such a claim would require a pro-feminist critique of patriarchy and an unpacking of male privilege. Instead, MTI draws from mestiza consciousness by making connections to specific aspects of this theory, such as the utilization of border crossing and liminal identities, negotiations of ambivalence and contradictions, as well as the use of a multiple consciousness for navigating multiple cultural worlds. Thus, although my focus here is exclusively on heterosexual males, I contend that an analysis of subjugated knowledge requires a serious consideration of theories, such as those from Chicana feminists, which have paved the road in articulating and exposing the ways of knowing among marginalized groups (e.g., Delgado Bernal, 2001; Delgado Bernal, Elenes, Godinez, & Villenas, 2006; The Latina Feminist Group, 2001; Zavella, 1991). Moreover, in drawing on Chicana feminist theories to study men, I wish to break the boundaries of relying solely on male-centered scholarship. This, I believe, is in line with the spirit of Anzaldúa's notions of border crossing and social justice through scholarship, albeit with humility, transparency, and critical reflexivity.

Moving towards a Mestiz@ Theory of Intelligences encompasses a conceptual leap from a history and scientific tradition that resulted in marginalization and discrimination for many Latin@ students. The intelligences debate has a long and problematic history. In the early part of the 20th century, the hereditarianism movement, which contended that individual differences in human beings, including intelligence, altruism, and aggression, could be primarily attributed to the basis of genetics and thus racial and ethnic groups, gained in popularity (Valencia, 2002). Moreover, the Stanford-Binet Scale, a cognitive-based test that estimated the intellectual capacity of children by comparing it with that of "normal" children and adolescents of various ages, became widely adopted and accepted as a valid measure to classify children based on IQ scores despite its obvious limitations when used with children from diverse backgrounds (Kincheloe & Steinberg, 1997). In the 1970s and 1980s, some of the psychometric measures related to testing were questioned, but the overall tracking of Latin@s into low academic tracks continues to this day (Carter & Segura, 1979). Intelligences and notions of "smartness" (Hatt, 2007) are often connected to positionalities that embody middle-class and whiteness-centric identities (Ford & Harris III, 1994; Hatt, 2011). Therefore, whiteness serves as the ideological mirror by which the "other" (student of color) is measured. Along these lines, Hatt (2007) points out that "overwhelmingly, it is poor and/or students of color who are unjustly left feeling not smart in schools through practices such as tracking and teacher expectations" (p. 2). Interestingly, Latin@s who gain access to high performing academic tracks in K–12 schools often experience strong tensions due to deficit discourses. Thus, they are seen as engaging in "smartness trespassing" by academically excelling in ways that are not perceived as typical from their ethnic group (Carrillo & Rodriguez, 2016).

There is a historical context that has triggered certain intelligences for survival and the pursuit of excellence in multiple domains. In fact, since the annexation of Mexico's northern territories (in the mid-19th century) by the United States, the Mexican American/Chican@ populations have had to navigate liminal identities (Elenes, 2011). Hence, the history of Mexican-origin students is one of psychic, spiritual, and cultural hybridity. I attempt to hone in on this concept as a complex sense of being in multiplicity that serves to negotiate various aspects of schooling and every day life. In conceptualizing MTI, I draw from extensive literature that offers prospects for understanding how one's social location (specifically as it relates to marginalized populations) can result in intelligences and "gifted" identities that are not adequately captured by MI theory or IQ tests. These gifts draw from border-crossing identities that illustrate flexible and elaborate cognitive acts that work in very hybrid ways. For instance, some Latin@ immigrant children serve as "gifted" cultural brokers (Valdés, 2003) from an early age when they assist their parents during various interactions within U.S. society. Many low-income Latin@ students negotiate streets smarts and book smarts (Conchas & Vigil, 2012; Lopez, 2002) and embody Latin@-centric *funds of knowledge* (Moll, Amanti, Neff, & Gonzalez, 1992), all while still attending to the needs of mainstream cultural capital found in K-12 schools. Further, there are Chican@ activist educators that "play the game"[8] (versus selling out) through strategies to work the system so that they can assist in supporting issues that affect oppressed communities (Urrieta, 2009). Additionally, many low-SES Latin@ students often use a *nepantla* (in-between) *consciousness* (Anzaldúa, 1987) and a *differential consciousness* (Sandoval, 2000) to identify, address, and negotiate various contexts, situations, contradictions, and ambivalences in their everyday lives.

These creative and talented improvisations are often overlooked and not conceptualized as intelligences. This work looks at how MTI is utilized by scholarship boys in ways that demonstrate intelligences that are different from Gardner's MI framework. I argue that dominant accounts of "intelligence" are situated within cultural productions informed by elements of power, ideology, politics, and the historical location of subjects. In other words, it is not an objective act to historically position students of color as not being among the most "intelligent." I have not known Gardner to use examples of working-class racial minorities to exemplify MI theory. For Gardner, his search for "intelligences" often consists of identifying the knowledge and performances of cosmopolitan elites.

MTI is an elaborate navigation system. Examining the ontological straddling of scholarship boys within MTI is a particularly important area of inquiry, especially in light of scholarship that connects working-class masculinities with counter-school attitudes (Foley, 1990; Willis, 1977). MTI coincides with one of Gardner's (2006) foundational definitions of what constitutes intelligence:

> An intelligence entails the ability to solve problems or fashion products that are of consequence in a particular setting or community. The problem-solving skill allows one to approach a situation in which a goal is to be obtained and to locate the appropriate route to that goal. (p. 6)

MTI is made up of the following strands: navigating/contesting oppression; centering subaltern knowledge; centering critical, hybrid identities; straddling multiple forms of cultural capital; decolonization; struggling for psychic, cultural, emotional, and spiritual wholeness; and remaining committed to social justice. In order to make a clear distinction from MI theory, I explain the various elements that make up MTI.

Navigating/Contesting Oppression

Various studies have examined the oppressive conditions faced by many Latino males that live in low-SES settings (Conchas & Vigil, 2012; Rios, 2011). This strand of MTI illustrates how these conditions can be negotiated through identities that navigate and contest oppression via creative and empowered strategies. This ongoing problem solving requires critical reflection, as well as mental, spiritual, and emotional endurance. Moreover, this intelligence helps to mediate feelings of the hopelessness and despair.

Centering Subaltern Knowledge

Centering knowledge that comes from "below" or from the margin is another important component of MTI. As Cammarota (2008) points out in his own ethnographic work on Latin@ students, linear assimilation into dominant culture and knowledge claims "…will probably not be sufficient to mitigate tensions of severe oppressive forces that limit opportunities and well-being. To make the best of a bad situation, young Latin@s must creatively draw from a variety of cultural resources and strategies to maintain their dignity, positive sense of self, and hope for a better, more beneficial future" (p. 13). In many ways, "keeping-it-real" and "not selling out" by centering subaltern knowledge is used as a political philosophy that strengthens a commitment to social justice and elevates the prospects for academic success. It is not a negative trait, but a more "authentic" positionality considering the hybrid lives and diverse cultural worlds that many low-SES Latin@ students inhabit. This claim/notion differs from the dichotomies inherent to research that suggests that fears germane to "acting white" and a working-class habitus can derail academic goals for minority students and working-class males (Fordham & Ogbu, 1986; Willis, 1977).

Centering Critical, Hybrid Identities

In some ways overlapping with other components of MTI, this strand emphasizes the implications of living in hybridity and from a critical orientation. As such, this idea draws heavily from Anzaldúa's (1987) notion that Mexican origin people live in a borderland state that is engulfed in contradiction, ambiguity, and *nepantla* states of consciousness. Intelligences inherent to this type of hybridity reject ideas related to the need for bodies and minds to be forced into bounded notions of middle/upper-class/elite and Eurocentric models of the educated person. Moreover, this also speaks to the merits of using MTI as a core basis for conceptualizing intelligences amongst various Latin@ communities.

Straddling Multiple Forms of Cultural Capital

A key piece of MTI pertains to how intelligences are not bounded and separate ways of knowing, but instead multifaceted positionalities that interact with the needs and situations across class, race, ethnicity, and gender. This aspect coincides with work done on African American students and the notion of "cultural straddlers" (Carter, 2005); the reconceptualization of cultural capital (Yosso, 2006), which emphasizes the community cultural wealth embedded within various communities of color; and "cultural organizing," (Cammarota, 2008), whereby Latina/o youth "…glean resources from a variety of sources—both dominant and subordinate—to organize the conditions and experiences of life to better suit the human drive for creativity and self-determination" (p. 10). The Mexican-origin ghetto nerds in this work exemplify this trait from a young age.

Decolonization

Excelling academically is in part driven by a search for decolonizing knowledge and a creative resistance strategy that aims at achieving a continuous and reflexive decolonization process. Here, I draw from Walter Mignolo's (2007) ideas:

> De-coloniality, then, means working toward a vision of human life that is not dependent upon or structured by the forced imposition of one ideal of society over those that differ, which is what modernity/coloniality does and, hence, where decolonization of the mind should begin. The struggle is for changing the terms in addition to the content of the conversation. (p. 459)

This stance produces sometimes painful but also empowered identities that aim at staying "true" to community and the historical self all while pursuing mainstream demands in school. This strand also aligns well with the question that Cammarota (2008) suggests reflects a salient concern for young Latin@s: "what if he or she covets self-authenticity while simultaneously striving for academic success?" (p. 6).

Struggling for Psychic, Cultural, Emotional, and Spiritual Wholeness

This strand connects well with many of the other strands that make up MTI. Carrillo (2010) and others (Urrieta, 2009; Valenzuela, 1999) have pointed out that achieving academic success within *whitestream* (Urrieta, 2009) schools often creates all sorts of tensions and identity struggles for many low-SES Latin@ students. Intelligence relates to emotional and spiritual wholeness, extending beyond traditional notions of education. Coming from marginalized spaces often illuminates knowledge about how schooling can be just an academic exercise that is devoid of holistic growth. This intelligence is also about contesting Cartesian notions of mind-body splits.

Remaining Committed to Social Justice

This strand posits that achieving high levels of formal schooling is an important way to achieve social justice goals. The knowledge, resources, and cultural and social capital that is attained by pursuing higher education is perceived as a valuable tool for pushing for equity in communities of origin, schools, knowledge production, and in the larger society. As such, "success" is problematized and removed from bounded, linear, individualistic definitions. Further, a commitment to social justice complicates the notion that credentials (degrees, diplomas) and access to higher levels of consumption power equates with "making it."

MTI and Scholarship Boys

In part, MTI draws from the work on scholarship boys. For Hoggart (1957/2006), his conceptualization of the scholarship boy pertains to the "uprooted and anxious" identities of working-class students who excel academically. Scholarship boys often experience intense "hidden injuries of class" (Sennett & Cobb, 1972) and nostalgia as it relates to their working-class roots. While an important contribution, Hoggart's notion of the scholarship boy did not take into account the intersectionality of race, ethnicity, and class. It was not until Rodriguez (1975, 1982) wrote about his scholarship boy experiences that specific connections were made to Latin@s. His work has gathered both acclaim and significant backlash for some of his views related to issues such as bilingual education, multiculturalism, and assimilation. For Rodriguez, there is a necessary dichotomy between the public and private selves. In contrast, for the scholarship boys in this research, these worlds merge, and are centered as primordial examples of complex, "authentic," and multicultural ways of being, knowing, and surviving the subtractive aspects of schooling. Moreover, Rodriguez's take on the scholarship boy is largely influenced by a more privileged private-school experience in a K-12 school. The present work differs significantly in that it focuses on the experiences of barrio boys who attended low-SES public schools in urban settings.

Throughout this chapter, I use *ghetto nerd* (Diaz, 2007) interchangeably with scholarship boy to center the "gifted" working-class identities of academically successful Mexican-origin male students.

NEGOTIATING MULTIPLE WORLDS: MTI AND PORTRAITS OF MEXICAN GHETTO NERDS

> For it is a very different matter, and results in a very different intelligence, to grow up under the necessity of questioning everything – everything, from the question of one's identity to the literal, brutal question of how to save one's life in order to begin to live it. (Baldwin, 1985, p. 516)

When critically examining research on scholarship boys, I began to see how the intelligences of Mexican-origin ghetto nerds received minimal attention. Beyond class anxieties, there is an immense research gap that fails to account for the skilled border-crossing gifts of Mexican-origin scholarship boys. Here, I provide portraits of the Mexican-origin scholarship boys – David, Carlos, and Mario[9] – by making direct connections to MTI in ways that illustrate specific strands of this theory. I connect each case to two salient strands of MTI and I conclude by connecting all of the cases to how they remain committed to social justice. In order to offer context, I begin this section with brief biographies of each ghetto nerd.

David is a professor emeritus at a top-tier university located in the southwestern U.S. He is one of the pioneers of Chican@ studies and continues to engage in activist work. He grew up in two urban areas in the southwestern U.S., and he earned a PhD from a prestigious liberal arts university located on the west coast.

Carlos is an assistant professor of human development at a university located in the southwestern U.S. He was raised, as he puts it, at the crossroads between "poverty and sin." He attended public schools in a low-income neighborhood with mostly Latin@ and African American students. Carlos now teaches at the university where he earned his undergraduate degree. His research, activism, and scholarly commitments are to the Latin@ migrant community.

Mario is working on a doctoral degree in Curriculum and Instruction at an elite university located in the southwest. Like all of the scholarship boys in this work, he attended a public school that primarily served urban, low SES students. He is a former public school teacher and is now an administrator at a middle school in his community where he grew up. Mario is a community activist and was inspired early in his life by the work of Saul Alinsky and

Cesar Chavez as well as by the inequities that the Latin@ community experiences in his home state. Additionally, as stated earlier, each ghetto nerd examined in this chapter is a heterosexual Mexican American/Chicano male who is currently married with children.

David: Navigating/Contesting Oppression and Centering Subaltern Knowledge

> *It is important for you to be a scholar-activist, otherwise the colonized mind is alive and well.* (David)

David has a long history of contesting oppression and centering the knowledge of his Mexican American/Chican@ community. He is a key figure of the Chicano movement. His personal journey consists of contestations over his agency in the midst of hegemonic conditions. He reflects:

> I graduated from a barrio school as an honor student, a smart Mexican I thought. It was 1968. I did not know at the time I was victim of a vulgar tracking system. I got straight As but I did not get all the requirements for the UN (pseudonym for top-tier university system in his home state) campuses. So I had to go to the community college.

Tracking, which has been a salient feature of the urban, low-SES schooling experience for many Latin@s, helped to develop David's critical consciousness and assisted him in confirming his argument that Mexican-origin people live in an "internal colony" within the U.S. David has often had to deal with various forms of racism. He has been questioned for parking his car in the faculty area and has been categorized as a "foreigner" during faculty meetings when he is sometimes asked, "what part of Spain are you from?" According to David, "capitalism and white supremacy have nurtured sexism, racism, and homophobia." He often mentioned his association with "revolutionary" thought and his various readings of Gramsci and other critical thinkers. His active involvement in the Chicano movement had him on the front lines of the scholarly and protest side of politics and social change.

David wrote one of the classic, foundational books in Chicano studies, even amidst immense roadblocks including various publishers that did not want to publish his work. Thus, his use of MTI consists of centering the knowledge of his Chican@ experience. Moreover, his source of inspiration, as an "intellectual warrior," is a sense of being that is connected to the Chican@ community. In many ways, David remains committed to navigating oppression by speaking out against it at his university campus and in the community at large. Gardner fails to address these types of intelligences. This neglect occurs even as Gardner (1999) suggests that each intelligence evolves in an effort to deal with certain conditions in the everyday world (p. 95). David reflects on the complexity of his journey and his role in the academy. He comments:

> I have long asked myself the big question, which is: what am I, an activist, doing in the academy anyhow? We did not have a critical mass within the structure, but I made it through, because I was present in a historic moment. Institutions serve the state. Their historic role is to produce intellectual elites. Their historic role is to perpetuate the myth of Democracy and simultaneously reinforce the Eurocentric culture.

By committing to Chican@ causes and scholarship, he centers his subaltern positionality and finds a way to excel within mainstream institutions. He believes that many new Latin@ scholars are compromising their integrity by becoming part of certain cliques and publishing circles. His advice is:

> Think about your contribution as a public intellectual that speaks truth to power. Be your own man and woman but have the audacity to speak truth to power. You have to publish within the realities of the institution in mainstream journals. But also publish in other places.

Being his "own man" seems to entail that he fights back against cliques and structures that reproduce white privilege and do not attend to the needs of marginalized populations in the U.S.

As a barrio boy from the streets of two urban southwestern cities, David also did not compromise a certain kind of "urban-barrio-cool aesthetic" as he navigated *whitestream* (Urrieta, 2009) universities. His notion of "keeping it real" and opposing the status quo, including certain forms of authority, have not led to anti-learning sentiments or stalled schooling achievements. His nuanced ghetto nerd male identity seeks to use power and privilege as a faculty member to speak his notion of "truth" to the hegemonic state. Knowledge is crucial for speaking out and molding arguments that reflect his views of social justice. While he no longer has the knees to play basketball with students at the university gym, he remains young in spirit based on his ideals. He tells me:

> The love, you know, it conquers all. With the love you speak truth to power…I do not feel my age. The struggle keeps me strong. Keeps me young. People get burned out with the struggle. Life is struggle and struggle is life.

Additionally, David was moved by the power of marginalized knowledge that speaks to eliciting social change. He became part of that voice and was also inspired by other organic intellectuals[10]. He reflects:

> I was inspired you know, by Antonio Gramsci. His *Prison Notebooks* (Gramsci, 1971). He wrote on toilet paper. I am going to prepare myself to do the same things, but I have to be a real smart Mexican. I wanted to be a real smart Mexican…

David is a "real smart Mexican" and remains committed to centering subaltern knowledge and fighting against oppression. His own decision-making and reflexivity illustrate how MTI is a politicized identity that informs a life-management system that assists ghetto nerds with dealing with oppressive conditions. Moreover, David has entered the academy as a barrio boy, and positions himself in some ways like Rodriguez (1982) when he states: "I have stolen their books. I will have some run of this isle" (p. 1). David's run of the isle pertains to learning and creating a knowledge canon that takes him out of the margins. He makes a deal with himself by naming the pain and silences, committing to loving his people, and engaging in a revolutionary praxis.

Carlos: Straddling Multiple Forms of Cultural Capital and Centering Critical, Hybrid Identities

> *Within those measurements of intelligence there is an implicit theory of being. Shit you pick up in school. When it comes to one's nature, these measurements would not understand that.* (Carlos)

Carlos grew up wondering if his smartness would ever be cultivated after his promising elementary school years. From middle school on, he was criminalized and silenced by an overt and hidden curriculum that failed to name his intelligences and as such, endorse his form of hybrid and embodied multifaceted humanity. He comments:

> There are people who are truly different yet we are all put in one system. Not everyone fits the norm. It's like crossing the border, going from one country to another.

In that border-crossing exchange, we have the development of a new consciousness, where the order of things including dichotomies and linear truths are reworked to respond to tense ambiguities and subtractive schooling conditions. Carlos had an internal voice that told him that he was "smart," but, often times, it was something that was silenced in public spaces. He addressed this issue:

> So I go through the system knowing I am smart, but I am not recognized. Other people are recognized, but you know that is flawed. I stayed in school because I had some ideas, come on, I know I do, even though I did not get the respect. I was in palm-pilot mode for many years. I was told in some ways to not believe in myself.

Many Latino males are not recognized. That is, there are discontinuities and animated voices where our forms of smart may or may not be part of the teacher's gaze. Even for the "winners" of the schooling sweepstakes, such as the scholarship boys in this research, there is a sense of being made peripheral. Carlos has to force himself into intellectual existence. Much of this came from his connection to the library, he explains:

> But the book [Steinbeck's *Grapes of Wrath*] is cool because it allows us to 'not know.' Shit, it even allows us to be stupid and circle words like rivulet and dissipated. That gets at the allied nature you allude to. Only an ally, a true ally in your self-development would allow you to stop mid-sentence and tag them up. *Neta*, that's the frame I see it through. The library as the ally.

In the library, like at the gym, he worked out and sought out critical forms of scholarship and literature. He also uses his form of MTI to contest discourses related to his brilliance by seeking out books that reminded him that he "was smart again." The home knowledge, community knowledge, and the strategies that come from being ignored or deemed second rate are also key pillars for intellectual growth. Carlos explains his predicament:

> I knew how to interpret, inform, hypothesize like any white student. Schools are not really good in general at tapping at resources we bring to the table. That shit my *abuelita* (grandma) taught me, I could never bring that to school.

Carlos knew he was intelligent, but he experienced the racial, class, and gendered aspects of marginalization. Schools and teachers positioned him as a Latino male body that was not intelligent. In some ways, this challenged his interest in schooling (but not learning). Nurturing a working-class, Mexican-origin notion of a reasonable man of letters required that Carlos seek out the library because in K–12 schools he experienced deficit thinking. In fact, the gender and racial script in most of his K–12 schools entailed that people who looked like him were considered "dumb" or "trouble-makers." He told me once about how unexpected it was for someone like him, with his barrio posture and "look," to sit on the floor in the library for hours, sometimes twice a day, putting in the "work of the mind." In this way, his positionality is about men getting power through intellect and developing resistance to discourses in schools that frame Latino men as dangerous and intellectually inferior to white people. This is different from some of the studies on working-class men that have found that they develop full-blown counter-school attitudes due to various gender and class discourses within schools (Rios, 2011; Willis, 1977). He consistently had to negotiate these various forms of cultural capital, those that he brought with him to school as a barrio boy and the expectations of mainstream schools. Describing his college experience, he told me: "I loved being in class and having the chance to serve them." "Serving" is a term that symbolizes power as it reflects his ability to put people in check, to inform the "misinformed," and to educate.

For Carlos, centering his belief in being a smart student became an ongoing battle. He elaborates on the intersectionality of race and ethnicity and "smartness":

> I knew I was special. I felt special. I knew I was not slow. A lot of it was race and that we were not as well liked in middle school and high school compared to white peers. Things changed after elementary school. Being in a classroom you want your smartness cultivated, but later you are not invited to the party. So you develop all sorts of responses to address this mistreatment.

According to Kimmel (1996), men make themselves within a historical and social context. For Carlos, his critical, hybrid identity pushed him to create spaces in which he could "remember" that he was intelligent. MI theory fails to account for the intelligences that Mexican American scholarship boys possess as a consequence of their upbringing in a bicultural context and experiences of class mobility. Carlos was never told he should apply for college while in high school. In fact, the journey that led to him to earn a PhD at a top-tier research university started in a very tragi-comedic and inspirational way. One day, not long after his high school graduation, he rode his bike from his barrio community to a little hill. From there, he saw a community college and became absorbed by the idea that he could attend this place of "higher learning." Inspired, he bought a backpack and applied for financial aid. Initially, he thought his dream was shattered when he read that his expected family contribution was 90 dollars. He thought he had to come up with that money. After realizing that this was not going to be the case, he enrolled in college, and went on to earn stellar grades. He explains that once at the doctoral level: "I did really well for myself. I was top of my class; nobody can take that away from me." His current struggles with politics in the academy and his quest for, as he puts it, "doing meaningful work" kept him busy. He straddles his work with the migrant community, his notion of "barrio truth," various discourses and expectations from within the *whitestream* academy. In the midst of all this, he continues to excel in his own ghetto nerd way. He recently was awarded the most prestigious fellowship in his field.

In the end, Carlos embodies the positionality of a gifted border crosser. His use of MTI encompasses ongoing improvisations and mastery of multiple cultural worlds. His experiences demonstrate that "racially stigmatized masculinities" (Lopez, 2011) require that power and resistance be negotiated through culturally situated and flexible responses. Moreover, the "disadvantages" (Anyon, 1997) that are part of the journeys of those who attend "ghetto schools" are mediated by elastic and hybrid mobilization of cultural capital and critical identities. He was able to maneuver and negotiate the expectations within different social-class contexts and network across class lines. This crossing of mind, heart, and soul interacts with class, gender, race, ethnicity, and history. This maneuvering is creative and often in opposition to the status quo. As such, mestizo bodies often draw creative and powerful forces. Pérez-Torres (2006) makes this point quite well: "mestizo subjects carry their body through globalized circuits of exchange. As part of this process, new identities are forged, new relations founded, new epistemologies undertaken in an innovative and inventive process creating new knowledge" (p. 215). The knowledge that stems from hybridity helped Carlos to survive and accomplish his goals within school, community, and beyond. Moreover, this use of MTI pertains to knowing that the hegemonic politics of "smartness" (Hatt, 2011) requires a forceful battle in the name of the holistic, empowered, and "intelligent" self. One has to know what is going on to then navigate the myths and toxic affects of social constructions designed by *whitestream* institutions and dominant knowledge structures.

Mario: Decolonization and Struggling for Psychic, Cultural, Emotional, and Spiritual Wholeness

Being smart does not get you to graduation, being a puppet does. (Mario)

According to Paulo Freire (1974), "critical consciousness is integrated with reality; naïve consciousness superimposes itself on reality; and fanatical consciousness, whose pathological naïveté leads to the irrational, adapts to reality" (p. 39). For Mario, his journey started in a low SES community, made up mostly of Latin@ and African American students. His critical perspective on schooling and sensemaking of "reality" results in intense battles with the expectations of having to assimilate into the status quo. In his words, "many middle-class whites and High-spanics (sold-out Latin@s)," have an easier time "making it" and graduating. He framed these students as puppets of the status quo. His negotiation was with a dominant class that he believed violently expected assimilation into its cultural expectations around individualism, competition, linear and Eurocentric notions of schooling, and middle-class tastes. Similarly, the scholarship boy, Richard Rodriguez (1982), reminds us that schooling is not a natural human endeavor:

> Haunted by the knowledge that one chooses to become a student. (Education is not an inevitable or natural step in growing up.) Here is a child who cannot forget that his academic success distances him from a life he loved, even from his own memory of himself. (p. 48)

For Mario, like Rodriguez, education became the polemic site of rewards and significant separation from the life he lived as a kid. He engaged in strategic invisibility in an effort to seek wholeness on his terms. In this sense, he sometimes purposely did not meet deadlines, ignored emails from faculty, or failed to show up to graduate-student functions, in the name of seeking critical distance, reflexivity, and authenticity on his own terms. Also, Mario has had to negotiate the tensions of "rising up" according to dominant society's notions of success, while trying to hold on to "the past" and an initial working-class consciousness that groomed his resistance to the "norm." Part of his intelligence work encompassed working through the dimensions of his identity that nurtured his understanding of how to perform the rituals of academic success, all while respecting his family, "culture," and knowledge that came from his ghetto nerd experiences. For Mario, this is a psychological and spiritual fight that deals with ethics, love, and the aesthetics of seeing strength and beauty in those aspects that middle America tells Latin@s to "leave behind." He sees most people as co-opted by a false and dehumanizing vision. In contradiction, Mario strives for those things that are sometimes ignored by schools: humility, a counter-efficiency identity, an anti-competition ethos that includes intimacy, love, care, and community.

This, according to Mario, is a painful, confusing, and ongoing internal dialogue. He exposes the dialectical structures that shaped his experiences all while decolonizing himself by challenging metaphors that he felt were subtractive. He also has had a long history of questioning his teachers. He told me:

> I remember social studies with a coach as a teacher. He had biases. When he brought up Columbus, I was like: how does it make sense for me to come to your house and say I discovered you? He got offended. You know, white folk, they center themselves sometimes and tell us the history. When we shoot back, they get nervous. I began to think about why Latinos quit school. You cannot have an intelligent conversation in public schools bro. I was suspended for insubordination.

In this context, where he identified minoritized populations as being exploited by Anglos, he began to see, as he often says: "the world as it is, versus the world as it should be" (he draws from Saul Alinsky). He read all the ethnic studies literature he could get ahold of and also became trained in community organizing. He also saw the southwest as a colonial space where, as he puts it: "white men with rifles still make up the statues in our universities and neocons[11] in the legislature are clueless about our needs." In Mario's analysis, his state of residence is tainted with policy decisions informed by white supremacy, deficit thinking by teachers, systemic racism, and a historical agenda informed by Manifest Destiny. Hence, his views about becoming an educated person are informed by a macro world that positions Latin@s as the other.

To seek wholeness, he sometimes ignores emails from faculty committee members or takes semesters off. He sees this as a way to get a PhD his way, even if it means taking a little longer. Also, he is at odds with having to get approval for his writing. His struggle is intense:

> Oh man, I feel it on a daily basis. It's like this. If I do not finish my doctorate, this is the reason why: I have to make a choice. The choice is: how much of me will be left? It will not be because I cannot meet the academic standard or because of will. No! Nah, it has to do with the me of yesterday and the one they are trying to create today…seriously, when I write a paper, I have to fit into the norms of the middle class. If I do it all just to move up, it is not worth it…every time you lie to your heart, you erase yourself.

When thinking through this comment, Mario poses the complexity of intellectual masculinities facing issues of class, gender, and history. He mentioned to me that he did not want to be a "poser" or "whited out", but that he also refused to stay away from mainstream institutions of higher learning. He constantly questioned where he should live, how he should pursue his life, and what goals were worthy for a Latino male that was seeking to be decolonized. He lived in the same barrio community where he grew up and found this to be one cornerstone of his toolkit that made him feel like he was not selling out. Yet, he believed in the dream of getting a doctoral degree and having access to the power that may come with it. He drove many hours or got on an airplane just to attend class He refused to be fully immersed in the college student role, but does not leave the process entirely. Mario stayed close to his community, always reflected in critical ways, and creatively found ways to not fully lose himself in the achievement discourse so that his notion of wholeness and dignity were kept intact. His embodiment of MTI clearly illustrates how "…competing and compelling forces pull the mestizo body – and its sociocultural significance – in different directions. Or perhaps, more abruptly, the mestizo body moves in multiple directions as it enacts numerous, frequently contradictory, discourses of identity" (Pérez-Torres, 2006, p. 46). This pull of hybrid agency is deeply contextual, intersectional, painful, and often elicits new questions and possibilities.

Sometimes he battled through depression for a short time and was ready to get back into the "game" rather quickly. Other times it was about resistance by way of ontological recluse. He isolated himself and broke down internally. He eventually designed strategies for seeking the justice that is not easily and openly available in the spaces where he attended school and in his own position as an administrator at an urban middle school. For instance, when schooling became problematic, he would take semesters off or slow down the process of his dissertation writing. He caught his breath and began to create a strategy for how to continue his studies without fully becoming hyper-immersed in the individualistic, competitive nature of academia.

Resisting hegemonic norms is part of the negotiations, but not the end of the story. Mario also had to work through some issues in his own community:

> Looking back, I should have just got a GED. My high school was a war zone. I wore two masks. One mask to pass the class and another to watch my back. Crazy fools were watching you. You had to kick it with them, those hanging outside. I had to be in switch mode, to survive. I learned that then, how to switch, and navigate all this information. You can identify the lie, the punk, the rawness of it all.

Mario wore multiple masks as he engaged a border-crossing consciousness. His dedication to the "rawness" exemplified his commitment to an identity as a ghetto nerd who rejected linear assimilation and struggled through the ambivalence of being and becoming. In one of the interviews, Mario told me: "we come from a different experience from the middle class. You will never see me at a Starbucks playing Sudoku. I can't get too comfortable, you know, I feel the pain and struggle every day." He navigated the tensions of being forced to become a puppet all while working through the various cultural worlds in his school. Moreover, that role-playing and switching became a permanent part of his scholarly ethos. He identified with the graffiti-filled alleys of life, the underdog, the maladjusted, and the forbidden knowledge, all while attempting to make sense of the more sanitized spaces of higher education and challenges in K–12. For Hoggart (1957/2006), feelings of "homelessness" are core feelings of the restless scholarship boy. In many ways, the road seems never to reach a place of tranquil sanctuary. In the colonial context under which Mario was schooled, there was always a confrontation with the various demands of domination. He embodied an existential, survival positionality. For Mario, resistance hurt, but obedience hurt more. Finding fluidity is challenged by chronic irresolution.

Gardner's (1985) MI theory fails to capture this complex dimension, one that is salient to many oppressed groups. It involves much more than mainstream notions of bodily and cognitive mastery. More is on the line, such as struggling for and having the opportunity to live a life of dignity. In this intellectually and spiritually demanding space, aims for wholeness and decolonization stir active and ongoing sets of intelligences that aim to critically examine and understand discourses, expectations, and knowledge claims surrounding the brown body within schools.

Mario utilizes MTI when he travels between different states of being. This is a clear example of how he embodies the Mestiz@ Theory of Intelligences. He crosses multiple worlds along race, ethnicity, and class. He assesses the needs in each context and makes critically conscious decisions. Part of the essence of working through MTI entails that there is psychic and spiritual unrest as he works through the violence of engaging Eurocentric ideas and norms in the larger society.

Being grounded in struggle is crucial to how Mario positioned himself as critical thinker and graduate student. He worked through MTI as he negotiated contradictions, ambivalence, and forms of ambiguity that are inherent to pursuing graduate study at an elite university in the United States. He engaged in critical reflexivity as he reflected:

> I know the norm is unjust in historical terms and has been oppressive to Latinos and does not relate to us. We can attach ourselves to it. We do it unconsciously sometimes, we follow the flow, but, I catch it. I see when I go into the sell-out category. Moving up is defined by whom? Knowledge is defined by whom? The dominant culture defines it, you don't move up until they give you the credentials and you follow their rules.

As outlined by this quote, Mario contends that oppression is the result of the pressure to uphold the values and expectations of the dominant society. He works through a borderlands identity that assists him in fighting through dichotomous and top-down metaphors that are expected for all those who are "rising up." In this space of struggle, he navigates a complex set of historical and discursive arrangements in search of holistic wholeness and decolonization. As he continues to ascend the academic latter, he remains committed to his mantra of: "…I don't want to lose that consciousness of coming back, of being real and making a true difference."

WEAVING THE PORTRAITS TOGETHER: A COMMITMENT TO SOCIAL JUSTICE AND EXTENDING MI THEORY

Similar to Urrieta's (2009) work on Chican@ activist educators, the ghetto nerds in this research "played the game" within whitestream schools with a "…strategic understanding of power and critical exertion of activist agency" (p. 33). They used this ability to enact social justice initiatives within their communities, the schools they attended, and their scholarship. Moreover, social justice drives an identity that situates knowledge and power as interconnected resources for changing the world.

This dedication to social justice is a salient trait of MTI. All of the Mexican-origin ghetto nerds in this chapter positioned themselves as intellectual and pragmatic "fighters" for social change. In many ways, their dedication to being on the "outside" of middle-class white male student "looks" (and positionality) speaks to what Mario described as: "…not becoming too white and then forgetting the purpose of all this and who you really are. I will never get comfortable."

Extending MI Theory

> Consistently, Gardner fails to see any threat from right wing power brokers who want to create Eurocentric schools that celebrate whiteness

> and patriarchy as the highest forms of civilization. (Kincheloe, 2004, p. 143)

I agree with Gardner's stance that human beings are intelligent in a plethora of ways. As MTI demonstrates, those "ways" extend far beyond MI theory. The portraits of the Mexican-origin scholarship boys in this research demonstrate that intelligences "from below" can add a mestizaje element absent in Gardner's MI theory. Moreover, while I do infer from my conversations and reading of Gardner's work that his desire to add complexity and equity to the intelligences debate is genuine, there still remain some significant blind spots inherent to his work. The decontextualized and objective claims in his theory help to solidify white privilege and, as a consequence, disenfranchise many low-SES students of color. It is important to culturally situate intelligences and be transparent about the role of power in identifying some students as smart and gifted and others as "dumb" or "not smart enough." As Berry (2004) points out, MI theory "reproduces the dominant, mainstream social, institutional, and civilizational structures of Western culture" (p. 237). MTI emphasizes the intellectual wealth and agency of those at the margins and positions them as having important sources of knowledge. In theorizing MTI as an embodied state of being, which is highly influenced by emotion, pain, struggle, and critical reflexivity, I am claiming that many Mexican American/Chican@ scholarship boys embody and perform holistic forms of intelligences that move away from Cartesian notions that claim that there is a mind-body split. MTI is, in part, the result of the "soul wounds" (Pizarro, 2005) of scholarship boys. Oppression, poverty, and segregated lives serve as a laboratory for the development of gifted identities.

When I attended Gardner's lecture on "Five Minds for the Future" at Harvard University on January, 12, 2012, I asked him if he had considered the connections between mestiza consciousness and intelligences among some marginalized populations. He was confused about what I meant by consciousness. As a psychologist, consciousness was really is not his area of inquiry. In addition, Gardner explained that he had never heard of Gloria E. Anzaldúa's work. I bring this up only to suggest that critical mestizaje and the border-crossing identities of the Mexican-origin scholarship boys in this research are not "named" or recognized by an MI theory that was created without their historical, cultural, and sociopolitical experiences in mind. In fact, "in research about intelligence and genius, Caucasian males are the dominant sample" (Kincheloe, Steinberg, & Tippins, 1999, p. 113). As such, MI theory is an important yet incomplete outline of human intelligence.

There are arguably inherent contradictions and issues in determining intelligence given that framing some individuals as intelligent and others as less intelligent is based on an imposition of paradigms. I do not claim to be outside of this tension, but do believe that since many scholars and school districts have made decisions that adversely affect many low-SES minority students in the world of intelligence politics and measurement, MTI could serve as one lens that may provide some alternative results. MTI has the potential to influence many teachers, administrators, and policymakers by providing a theoretical foundation to identify assets found in marginalized communities.

Limitations

While I do believe that MTI is a significant and important extension of MI theory, I am also conscious that this is an introductory analysis. I do not claim that this framework is free of limitations. The Latin@ population is a complex and heterogeneous group. Hence, I do believe that much work needs to be done within groups such as Puerto Ricans, Cubans, Guatemalans, and women, to see how this theory may or may not apply. As such, "the diversity of cultural styles, languages, and ethnic identities within the Latino American population needs to be recognized" (Conchas & Vigil, 2012, p. 63) within an MTI analysis. These portraits focused specifically on heterosexual, Mexican-origin men who were born and raised in urban spaces within the southwestern U.S. Female and queer students are also missing from this analysis.

My initial interest in this work came from reflecting on my own scholarship-boy journey. I wanted answers pertaining to the conflicting feelings that I had about "making it" within mainstream spaces and was interested in the cerebral and emotional work that it takes to cross so many literal and figurative borders. Hence, my decisions pertaining to the group I selected were largely influenced by my own experiences, passions, and evolving questions as a heterosexual scholarship boy of Mexican-origin who was raised in the barrios of southern Los Angeles. Moreover, I wanted to revisit the scholarship boy work done by Richard Rodriguez and apply this lens to urban males who attended low-SES public schools. In this view, all of the scholarship boys in this chapter were raised in low-income settings. In sum, these cases are important contributions to a discussion of how we can extend MI theory, and they point to the need of examining other regions and populations.

Implications for Schools

> Boys of color are often characterized in society as deficient. That is, they are stereotyped in ways that are detrimental to youths' self esteem. Often black and Latino men are viewed as a menace to society—drug dealers, gang bangers, lazy, loud, and dangerous…school reform efforts and policy should work hard to characterize boys of color as untapped assets—vital to their communities and society. (Conchas & Vigil, 2012, p. 133)

For the Mexican-origin ghetto nerds in this chapter, doing well in school was highly contingent upon how MTI was utilized and recognized as a tool for self-definition and empowerment. These heterosexual men used hybrid, critical identities that continued to shape their responses to oppression and highlighted the immense energy and gifted abilities necessary to negotiate multiple, and often contradictory, cultural worlds. As such, the reproductive function of schools was mediated and contested through critical, cultural, and systemic awareness.

MTI is an important tool for schools that aim at moving away from deficit-oriented approaches related to how Latino males and other marginalized populations are imagined. Teachers, principals, and other vested stakeholders could utilize MTI as a philosophical and pragmatic approach to education by identifying gifted students "in-context." Current uses of standardized tests, IQ exams, or "intelligent" performances that align with middle-class cultural capital remain insufficient. Professional development with honest and even painful discussions about MTI can assist in providing necessary ontological shifts and site-specific ways to frame curriculum, gifted-student identifications, policy, and ultimately contribute to the development of empowered identities among Latin@ students. In this way, interested stakeholders can begin to see Latin@s from an asset-based lens and thus invest in pedagogical, professional development, and policy models that are holistic and grounded in empowerment. Current ways of defining smart students has disenfranchised many Latin@s whose intelligence includes navigating through the educational system while seeking power and dignity in spaces outside of subtractive schooling environments.

While research suggests that Latino males are vanishing from U.S. higher education (Noguera, Hurtado, & Fergus, 2012; Saenz & Ponjuan, 2009), this work points to the importance of examining the schooling trajectories and identities of academically successful, low-income Latin@ students. In the end, schools (K–12 and higher education) should critically analyze the various dislocations with which Mexican-origin males grapple and begin to consider mestizaje, specifically MTI, as a potentially important toolkit that may help these students excel academically all while maintaining strong cultural identities.

NOTES

1 An earlier version of this chapter was published as: Carrillo, J. F. (2013). I Always Knew I Was Gifted: Latino Males and the Mestiz@ Theory of Intelligences (MTI). *Berkeley Review of Education*, *4*(1), 69–95.

2 During my first year as an assistant professor, I attended Howard Gardner's lecture (January 12th, 2012).

3 My use of "@" in Latin@ is an effort to be gender inclusive and to move away from the inherent sexism and assumptions of heterosexual normativity in the masculine term, "Latino." In solidarity with Asencio and Acosta's (2010) assessment concerning their use of the word, Latina/o, I use Latin@ to "…acknowledge equally the experience of women and men in the construction of this diverse and heterogeneous community" (p. 4). Latin@ is also useful for disrupting binary notions of identity cultural production. Some scholars have used other terms to explore these issues. For instance, Rodríguez's (2003) use of *queer Latinidad* also provides insight into "…the process by which constructions of identity work to constitute one another, emphasizing 'and' over 'is' as a way to think about difference. So, *latinidad* is about the 'dimensions' or 'the directions in motion' of history and culture and geography and language and self-named identities" (p. 22). Similarly, Latin@ Critical Race theorists (Cantú & Fránquiz, 2010) use Latin@ over Latino to center the heterogeneity among those of Latin American heritage and to utilize gender inclusive language. I use Latin@ as an umbrella term which covers groups such as Mexican American/Chican@ males, while still acknowledging the unique experiences of this group in comparison to other Latin@s.

4 While this work solely focuses on Latino males, I use the term "mestiz@" in order to leave the conversation open for those that may look into how MTI may or may not apply to women or those of non-conforming gender identities. I elaborate on some of these issues in the *limitations* section.

5 I use this term as a metaphor for negotiation multiple cultural worlds and identities.

6 Howard Gardner is a developmental psychologist and John H. and Elisabeth A. Hobbs Professor of Cognition and Education at the Graduate School of Education at Harvard University.

7 For Bourdieu (1984), cultural capital refers to a set of dispositions and cultural knowledge largely informed by or associated with one's social class. He contends that schools generally reflect and valorize the cultural capital of the middle and upper classes over those of the working and poor classes.

8 Playing the game in this instance refers to how some Chican@ students position themselves as having to participate in the expectations, dogmas, and value systems of the mainstream academic world, which is embedded in Eurocentric, middle class, individualistic, and Western values, in order to excel academically, without compromising (which would be seen as selling-out) socio-political and cultural values and commitments.

9 These are pseudonyms used to protect the privacy of participants.

[10] According to Gramsci (1971), organic intellectuals are individuals that come from a particular class/community context. In his view, they have the potential to counter hegemonic structures and ideologies.

[11] Neoconservatives. Although not neatly aligned with various views on this term, Mario is mainly referring to the extreme right-wing political infrastructure whose policies and symbols still make up a core part of his home state.

CHAPTER 6

REVISITING RICHARD RODRIGUEZ

> What preoccupies me is immediate: the separation I endure with my parents in loss. That is what matters to me: the story of a scholarship boy who returns home one summer from college to discover bewildering silence, facing his parents.
>
> (Rodriguez, 1982, p. 5)

Make it beautiful and honest. That is the voice that guides this chapter. Recently, I danced with my wife at the Maxwell concert. I am in love. You know, my wife; she glides through a dance move as blue light serenades the night and I am reminded of the way my parents raised a scholarship boy that comes home every once in a while—we also have incoherent silences and desperations. It is books, my moving away, my melancholic reflections, "education," it is all of that, as well little pieces of cheese at fancy receptions where I see spiritual reflections of my parents saying: *do not forget about us*. Education has been access and deception, redemption, and ambivalence. I once felt dead and education pushed me toward a public voice. Yet, all these words do not correct all the things that should have been. My parents still are in search of a "home" and demand that I give them money every time I see them. My father still walks over to his minivan to drink more and more beer: what happened to his hopes? Who did he want to become? We are a barrio family from the streets of Compton, Lynwood, and other south L.A. barrios. We have a lot of strength left. My parents left rural Sinaloa, Mexico for Los Angeles in the 1960's. We should be crying as we look through the photo album. Our "American Dream" took place in a cemetery.

This chapter revisits some of Richard Rodriguez's ideas related to the scholarship boy. As such, I will primarily cite his work as well as provide my own reflections. I break up this chapter into the following sections: "Moving Up," Language, and Memory.

MOVING UP

I guess all Mexican origin kids have a somewhat similar fate: a politician will tell them that they are invaders. A teacher will them that they are not part of the "civilized race" and that their group is not particularly "gifted."

A police officer may hit us (or more). Maybe, "just" insult us. I had to defend myself at early age and *read* violence while pondering: where is the love? In the barrio I used the violence directed at me to walk more blocks, to read more books, to synthesize a lot more. As a teenage student, I was the well-behaved scholarship boy full of pent up rage. It is just not natural to wake up, get out of my mother's hands, crawl, walk, and then have to dream in this context.

I see a car in the distance. A small, curvy road awaits the driver. I am walking near the Smoky Mountains in the state of North Carolina. The mountains seems to lean to the right. The stunning, lush green landscape and valley give me precious moments even as I struggle through a cold. In this terrain, the barrio boy "moved up" in elevation, but larger questions prevail. "Moving up" and social class mobility are premised on incomplete truths. Achievement and access are political terms. "Making it" or "moving up" are embedded in cultural agreements. I am not suggesting that having children, moving to place of opportunity is a bad thing. But, I agree with Rodriguez (1982) in that the scholarship boy shares a larger lesson: "…education is a long, unglamorous, even demeaning process – *a nurturing never natural to the person one was before one entered a classroom*" (p. 73).

For Richard Rodriguez (1982), gain was immersed in intense feelings of loss and separation. Excelling in school meant separation and distance from his working-class family. There was a loss of intimacy. He never completed his PhD. Loneliness set in. While in graduate school, Rodriguez was awarded a Fulbright Fellowship to study in London. But as he states:

> …then came the crisis. The domed silence; the dusty pages of books all around me; the days accumulating in lists of obsequious footnotes; the wondering doubts about the value of scholarship. My year in Britain came to an end and I rushed to "come home." Then quickly discovered that I could not. Could not cast off the culture I had assumed. Living with my parents for the summer, I remained an academic – a kind of anthropologist in the family kitchen, searching for evidence of our "cultural ties" as we ate together. (Rodriguez, 1982, p. 172)

Every time I get off an airplane to visit my parents: I think, "what are all the things that we never did as family?" My freshman year, I was studying at the University of the Michigan. I was never happy. A young lady from Michigan said she could show me how to pick out a jacket at the mall. A tall, nice guy, a student, told me that he could take me to his family's house for Thanksgiving. The snow fell on my wrists, I deciphered the wrinkles as family history, loss, and separation. The world that the scholarship boy wanted – love, unity, family, community, justice, peace, it was, for the most part, far away now.

And this distance increased every time I read a book. Incoherence increased the more access I had to the establishment. It was like I could see larger, inconvenient truths come to the fore. Perhaps moments matter – selling shoes at the swapmeet, watching my mother pick-up some food stamps, looking for my father at a bar and seeing him in jail. I reached for another world and it kind of came my way even as the love song was focused on another side of town. It remains a surreal dance even as more people that look like me are pushed to be "better" by entering higher education.

It is true. I have gone through three divorces. One was from my first wife. I still recall telling her that I wanted to go to graduate school in Florida. I got admitted. A few debates or arguments ensued, and before Christmas I was told to leave "home." At the time, I was the father of two young boys. The pain got me dizzy, nurture was somewhere, but this chapter was now violently closed. Second, or maybe this should be first; I left Compton, California in 1994 so that I could begin my college journey. Third, as a high achieving Chicano scholarship boy I began to deconstruct the myths around schooling and "success" much more deeply in graduate school. That divorce was about myth vs. "reality." My evolving truth is that the leaves that come down in the fall make North Carolina an excellent dance partner and narrator of truth. The little things move us up – conversations, helping out a person in need, falling in love again, and resting with some good music. *I am not afraid. I had to live. I have to live.*

Rodriguez (1992) contends that this nation was built on a fear of crowds. Puritans mainly trust the solitary life. I see the house on the hill. People build walls and fences. People dread encroachment of the supermarket. Or even more so, encroachment of the "other." Even "liberals" want to make sure you are the "right kind" of other. You know, we have to keep the property values up. We must follow the rules of engagement. In this tragicomedic journey of supposedly "moving up," these issues do come to the fore. Where should I live? I live with the "chusma" (loosely defined as a demeaning term for the working class), yet with middle class privilege. My neighbourhood supermarket does not sell organic food in any noticeable quantity. *There are a lot of processed peopled walking around.* The media says we have a high crime rate, prostitutes, and beat up motels in my 'hood. Across the street from my home, there is a new YMCA that is full of black and brown youth. I like that. When I check in, a young Latina, maybe 20, tells me that she is attending community college. She goes on to tell me that her grades were not too great last semester because someone stole her laptop. *I 'memer those days.* "Be careful," my wife's professor colleagues tell her. We are breaking the rules of "moving up." My fence is really low. Donald Trump probably would give it low marks. All are welcome, I guess. I buy a 7-dollar lock for the patio door. Hilarious. I come from the chusma. The prestigious fellowship and the library often equate with "away." With la chusma, I am in-kind of. My neighbour that works at Barnes and Noble does not know that I am writing this book. She helped me find a book once, that is all, and hi and bye. Part of me wants to die with a *capri sun* by my side, not organic cheese. Play Madonna really loud. Laugh: the bees will sting no matter where you live.

In the nearby vanilla suburbs I have access to tofu, a movie theatre, they steer away from "ethnic" candy, and there is a park that has a built-in miniature neighbourhood where my children can skate in "safety." There are no cars, only fences, and helicopter parenting and the nurturing of a protected childhood. It is all away from *la chusma.* I grew up with smog for lunch, drive-by shootings for dinner, and real helicopters roaming overhead during sleep hours. Perhaps Rodriguez (1992) is right in that the "…best resolution to the debate between comedy and tragedy is irresolution, since both sides can claim wisdom" (xviii). Maybe my suit is custom made in Rome. I walk with my wife at sunset alongside my Italian brothers and sisters as I crave a 7-Eleven Slurpee from a ghetto spot in Los Angeles. We are immersed in the creation of life. My son Emiliano is made in Rome and he is delivered in Chapel Hill, North Carolina: a Chicano-Italiano that will soon crave some *fixings*. *Molte Grazie* (many thanks).

There is some disappointment in arrival. But I still have the privilege to say that and still get an expedited security pass through the airport of my choice in the United States. I am California's son. A place Rodriguez (2013) contends passionately wrestles with discontent. *Oh what could have been.* The weather is so nice but the highways are too congested. "It is too expensive to live there," my Texas friends tell me. People like me, fantasize from a distance. I hit the books for so long. I am older now. My four year-old son quit T-ball after one inning of play. His eyes said, "this is boring and I am not doing no team chant!" He is showing early signs of discontent. Or perhaps, his demand for authorship is out in the open.

Mexico City. One of those trips that social class mobility has afforded me. I lean on Rodriguez (1992) when he states: "Mexico does not say it publicly but Mexico perceives America as sterile, as sterilizing, as barren as the nose of a missile. 'Don't drink the water in Los Angeles,' goes the joke, 'it will clean you like a scalpel'" (p. 91). I recall the Mexico City tourist guide telling our group that he disliked the rich side of town because it was "too American." So goes for Playa del Carmen (Mexico), my sister-and-law says, "they now have malls and stuff." I spot her expensive "American" purse that was purchased at a U.S. mall as she tells me this. Let us not become too *Americanized.* In that literal, symbolic, and contradictory space of imaginaries, desire and separation have a prayer. Assimilation is not a word for millenials. Now, we spread out from one location, we can be everywhere. Social media is a reminder of how my Mexicaness and scholarship boy journey is about boundary breaking all while knowing what kind of computer I want to hold on to. Fleetwood Mac and Eazy-E help me get clarity.

God, in the North Carolina stillness I pack my luggage and look for home. Adulthood tries to obligate me to "get over it." I went here, and there, and everywhere. Everything got moved around. And it is all, *still moving.*

LANGUAGE

> The common tongue of the oppressed was silence. (Kirkland, 2013, p. 58)

Beyond silence, some folk that are part of dominated groups accept the common sense of the hegemonic language order. But I am not blaming the "individual." My Chicano friend Dave drives his Honda Pilot through the Smoky Mountains in Western North Carolina and tells me: "Identity is hard. The colonial mind that conquest gave many of us – well, we don't even know who we are." The next day, a White North Carolinian, maybe 29 years old, tells me to go to Cherokee, North Carolina and spend some money in the casino that is there. He introduces me to his White girlfriend and his Mexican friend who is also dating a White woman. "And don't forget to try some squirrel!," he says. After forty minutes of chatter, we all hug it out, and he says, "y'all deep." My Chicano friend and I walk away. We are thankful for the encounter. This guy had a gentle soul and a distinct drawl: I did not see Mexico in him, but I did see a class connection: he saw himself as an outsider a bit. He was in a prison for a couple of years he told us. But being outside and inside, produces words that give me access to regions, to friends, to emotions. The school can be contested and the opportunity to live in linguistic hybridity is really, really, beautiful and just. I make more friends.

A standard language is often the result of war. Moreover, and problematically, in the U.S., bilingualism is often framed through ideas of "…language purism that demand that speakers perform two or more separate codes according to the hegemony of the 'standard' language (Garcia & Leyva, 2014), wether it be English or Spanish" (Cervantes-Soon & Carrillo, 2016). Beyond this, there are historical dynamics where Latin@ students have had to deal with deficit labels such as "handicapped," "mentally retarded," "at-risk," and "semilingual" (Flores, 2005). I share this backdrop in order to contextualize Rodriguez's (1982) infamous claim that there should be a separation between a private language and a public language. Spanish, he contends, is the language of the home. Bilingual Education is not something that he supports. In the U.S.-Mexican borderlands, where Rodriguez, myself, and the scholarship boys in this book came of age, war between the U.S. and Mexico nurtured a collision, systemic erasure, and ambivalence around what a border tongue means at home and in formal, mainstream contexts. As Rodriguez basically implies, only White children can have a merger between home language and the language that is taught in schools. Rodriguez makes his argument here:

> It is not possible for a child – any child – ever to use his family's language in school. Not to understand this is to misunderstand the public uses of schooling and trivialize the nature of intimate life-a family's 'language.' (p. 10)

Puro wiri-wiri. In other words, that is a lot of talk, elegant prose, but it is the poet's desire for romantic separation. I really like the way he writes and I thank him for paying for a nice lunch in San Francisco, California. But, sorry, shit happens, things mix. It is Rodriguez (2002) that reminds us that brown is where things will go. Blend. Language is no different. In North Carolina, I have met a lot of White youth that learned Spanish in Spain or Cuernavaca (Mexico). Their crossing of linguistic borders is often celebrated. For us working-class, public school kids, we also wanted to be bilingual. But, we live with a history that calls us sinners. Flores and Rosa (2015) make a relevant point:

> …raciolinguistic ideologies produce racialized speaking subjects who are constructed as linguistically deviant even when engaging in linguistic practices positioned as normative or innovative when produced by privileged white subjects. (p. 150)

There are racial categories and power dimensions that are orchestrated by the "White listening subject" (Flores & Rosa, 2015). This context is always at play, naming, and othering. *It is interesting that a subaltern tongue is rejected because of where it starts and a privileged tongue is accepted because of where it starts*. I could not go to Spain as kid. I could not afford it. But it was all right there in my barrio. The airport was not accessible and cosmopolitanism (in the mainstream sense) was denied for a minute there.

But as history shows us, the dark outsider "complains" and their truth and desires are embedded in labor history, invisible workers, not in authoring how things should be. My father falls from the sofa after drinking another beer. I am writing this book and he does not know. The television is too loud: Spanish blares out of the tv's speakers. Every time my father falls I have more to say about language, intoxication, and how working-class communities are stigmatized around their liquor stores and middle-class White neighborhoods brag about their breweries and craft beer. Language, privilege, power.

If *gringos* can eat tamales, I also want to proudly proclaim: "I am my language" (Anzaldúa, 1987). Rodriguez, in some ways understandably based on the historical moment in which he attended graduate school, was not firmly aligned with ethnic studies advocates. He did not receive in any extensive formal schooling in this area. For Rodriguez, language, specifically Spanish, was a reminder of home life and of the separation from public life and power. To me, you can be a citizen of the city and merge linguistic worlds and have this toolkit ready as needed. All of home life never really stays in the living room sofa. In fact, much of Rodriguez's power comes from vulnerability and willingness to share his "family's secrets." What we had and we lost provides a lot confusion. I want my freedom. I listen carefully to the sounds of loneliness and heartache: the scholarship boy is at his best when past and future, public and private merge and design dreams of love, beauty, compassion, and emancipation. My grandparents lived near a creek in Palmarito Mineral, Sinaloa, Mexico. I hear that water as I prepare to give a graduation speech. *That is relevant, that is not separation.*

Recently, I was in a restaurant in El Paso, Texas. A Latina, maybe in her 50's, asked me: "Mijo, are you in line?" I was not her son. But the combination of the Spanish, "mijo" with English, illuminated my version of Americanization. The intimate merger of private sounds with public life made the tacos taste a lot better. Moreover, Bettie (2003) notes that citizenship is associated with Whiteness: so why give this arrangement more power? I was schooled away from Spanish, but my *hunger of memory* and home life, kept it close, real close. I was able to maintain Spanish language proficiency while expanding what that exactly means. Nonetheless, I understand the pain, even the rage of being pushed out and trying to get in to say *something.*

Overall, it is clear that Rodriguez contends that the United States is very uncomfortable with making sense of mixing of any kind. He has optimism, even excitement at how people from various racial and ethnic groups fall in love and get married in places like California. So it is his writer's tease that provides contradictory messages about where and how things should be "separate" and not touch. The psychological costs of leaving home, of leaving Sacramento, California are still informing his ideas: that is the scholarship boy experience. The themes are always there: irresolution, contradictions, and the ongoing unpacking of the all the worlds that we inhabit and embody.

MEMORY

> Gatsby believed in the green light, the orgastic future that year by year recedes before us. It eluded us then, but that's no matter – tomorrow we will run faster, stretch out our arms farther.... And one fine morning – So we beat on, boats against the current, borne back ceaselessly into the past. (Fitzgerald, 1993, p. 115)

> …Mexican Americans have paid a price for the clarity of their past. (Rodriguez, 1992, p. 50)

Over lunch in San Francisco, California, Richard Rodriguez told me that his infamous book, *Hunger of Memory* (1982), is about class. For me, the book is about going to class, doing well, and entering another social class, looking back, playing games, getting injured in the process, loving more than before and it is also about movement, geography, sounds gained, sounds lost and changed. By looking back, there is mourning and respect. *Another person comes out on this side.*

I want to believe that I am bigger than my corner. But it is my corner that never leaves me. All those sounds, smells, emotions make I.Q. tests dizzy – kind of inside and outside of that there is a legit ivy league, right there, in the barrio. So many youth know what I am talking about. For Richard Rodriguez, the corner is static and no longer accessible and even suffocating. An ambivalence hits him. I get that, but the corner is love, completion of the journey, I honor it. I try. From there, all stories and communities are possible: *right there, I find love even when it hurts.* In fact, where stories collide there is often creation. In this contact between borders there is irony, tragedy, comedy, genius. You have to grab it, name it, and somehow get out of the Eurocentric propaganda that only sells escape (from our place of origin) and entry into their amusement park. Beyond binaries, the idea is that in the messiness there is a way to long for the past and emerge in the present.

I am not a minority – I am the *Great Gatsby*, Rodriguez seems to imply. One of my favourite lines from his work is, "I have taken Caliban's advice. I have stolen their books. I will have some run of this isle" (Rodriguez, 1982,

p. 1). Rodriguez despised the term minority. I am not a fan of the term myself. The larger question, or messiness, pertains to how the social and racial dynamics still adversely affect communities of color (even as scholarship boys get access to mainstream knowledge). As a Chicano scholarship boy I am at the crossroads of my life, school life, work life, and our "whole" life. I live between geographies and countries. Mexican pyramids do mean something to me. I do not forfeit a public life by watching my father fall of the sofa in the barrio.

I can't live my life without you. My most real life. In isolation I write, but really, I am in the crowd, the past gives me a bear hug and I take in all the Los Angeles smog. There are intelligences at work and pain comes to the surface. I have accepted and rejected my parents. Father, more than likely, you are wrong, I will not go blind because I read too much. Mother, the "Indian" is beautiful, I do not mind being in the sun and getting a little darker. My close friend Dave says that my mother is bipolar and a peer scholar during an undergraduate summer program at Princeton University told me that I should seek medical help because I speak in tangents.

If I never moved, I would not miss what I miss. Possibly. But in a southern porch, on a Los Angeles highway, over a Texan breakfast taco, I am reminded of the little Chicano kid that began reading his world and textbooks. My early years were rooted in the contrast between the noise of poverty at home and the silence and rituals of the robot schoolboy I was expected to be at my elementary school. My mother was constantly pissed off at my dad: *he was broke you know.* Still, we all laughed at how I read so much and at how my hands could not grab things with force. What kind of man was I going to become? My parents have rural roots and I am a city kid.

The way we lived as kids in working-class Los Angeles, California was embellished in intimate paranoia; it is like we ran into incompleteness together. The bills were never paid on time. But we did this together. There was a rush, an intimacy, a way to not check for asbestos, a way to know that that Beverly Hills was twenty minutes away. I applied for a college (undergrad) in a garage that had a light bulb with a long shoelace. My father slept on a little bed and told me to not tell my mother about the beer he had stashed back there. He drank and I wrote about why I should be accepted at the University of Michigan, Notre Dame, Georgetown, etc. My father became part of my personal statement – he was my co-author. The way we breathe is right there in the bag of Mexican sweet bread that my Tia (aunt) Noni brings from Mexico. I like sweets more than *Whole Foods* psychology because I am so mixed up and crave pleasure, even if it kills me in some ways.

All this writing reminds me of my mother counting her food stamps when I was at kid and at middle age, I check into my office at the University of North Carolina Chapel Hill, a crystal vision appears: the private family beginning informs the man I am today. I know what I love. My memories, these words, brings the private in touch with the public. *Strangers* email me. They want to talk about what I wrote. They also have memories. I walk up and down the hills of downtown Asheville, North Carolina and Appalachian sounds come from a band that is playing on a street corner: we all stand and listen, tourists and I. A lady that makes up the band clicks some spoons together. Wow. My friend Dave wants to go to McDonalds. He likes preservatives. The loneliness of the distance – Asheville to Compton is soothed by the conversations with locals that like my jokes and California stories.

When I wrote about the Mestiz@ Theory of Intelligences (MTI) in another part of this book I move some of Rodriguez's ideas into a different place. Distance merges, blends, with gifted possibilities. The barrio, the past, and the knowledge of the establishment converge, creating truly powerful and beautiful (and at times painful) cocktails. Remembering the past and what we learn through formal schooling structures pushes many Latin@ youth toward social justice goals. You do not leave "home" all the way. You bring it with you. That is Americanization, or one version of it. In many ways, this is a powerful form of critical cosmopolitanism that pushes back against binaries and bounded notions of assimilation. Moreover, this is what is possible and a counter-narrative to historically rooted deficit views toward Mexican families, which have been framed as providing a "simple" upbringing that impedes academic success (Gonzalez, 2014). Contrary to the arguments of some pundits, there is no "gold standard." But instead of escaping working-class culture and epistemologies, there is something to be said for being grounded in "all" worlds. That can be a legit Ivy League education.

Rodriguez (1992) contends that "Mexican Americans are in awe of education, of getting too much schooling, of changing too much, of moving too far from home" (p. 61). But, where I see the power of the Latino scholarship boy is in this: "…memory does not simply transmit information from the past to the present; it also transmits responsibilities" (Poole, 2008, p. 149). Further, Poole (2008) suggests that "it is because I have the kind of consciousness that places me in the past and also in the future, that a certain range of emotions and commitments become possible; I can have deeper and more satisfying relations with others than is possible for a being who does not have that kind of consciousness" (p. 162). Instead of dichotomous thinking, escape narratives, or communicating static nihilism: every minute delivers clarity, potentially, to fight for something that is bigger than the individual success journey.

THE WAY OUT IS IN

By going inside of memories, there is a more profound awe and access to a public world that merges multiple communities. Identity is always in motion and yet memory can provide commitment and responsibilities. In U.S. schools, many Latin@ students are not afforded the complexity and additive potential of memory. Instead, they are sold departure narratives that add to the confusion around family stories, community, history, and elevate White supremacy.

I do not have a recipe for all this. I was once a high school teacher. I am a father. I have been married twice. I do not like tofu but I do like a Starbucks caramel macchiato. This sentence is written on the east coast. Outside of the coffee shop window there is a road that leads to the Blue Ridge Parkway. My mother calls and worries that I may come across a bear. I am Mexican I remind her: I will not get up close and take a picture. My existential temperature is tempered today by the lighting and sunny, 85-degree weather. There are so many searchers in this town (Asheville, NC): they ask me about this book. Some say they can relate. So many of its residents that are under thirty of years of age have left "home." I wonder if I will have the chance to give them a copy of this book one day. Movement, prose, poetry, dialogue, pedagogy, philosophy.

I am left to think about issues like language. It is important to point out that *translanguaging* (Garcia & Leyva, 2014) is a form of dynamic bilingualism that disrupts language purism and offers hope for social practices and identities that center the subject in its enactment of diverse language practices. This perspective on language can provide Latin@ students with access to empowering notions of self, social justice ideas, and can lead to the development of a gifted toolkit of knowledge via the engagement and embodiment of multiple cultural worlds.

This is for all the scholarship boys and girls. When the Catholic Church in Rome, Italy rings the bell: I'll signal where the Pokemons are. For Richard Rodriguez and other scholarship boys, the journey is ambivalent, rewarding, layered with loss, and it is an ongoing assessment of academics, success, identity, and family. There are also layers around social justice and *freedom.* I have been to Big Sur, California. Mexico. My heartbeats remember: little towns where my grandparents came of age. Also, I grew up and learned about deportations of family members. I remember being in fear: an adolescent wrapped around his dreams—loneliness, hoping that I would be protected as I went for them. I was in love with learning and my parents, even when it was all full dysfunction. Growth maybe only happens when it is raining. I am still searching and moving. This paragraph is written near the Gulf of Mexico. I am in Texas feeling the breeze and daydreaming about southern California. It is summer and it is 6:00 am. A wave breaks in the distance. My daughter is about to wake up: she will want to get in the water. Faith, anxiety, and bird sanctuaries: *this has been a surreal process.*

What is done is done. The unsaid is known. The silence has words. I can hope. I gave so much to school. There are more questions than answers and I still fall asleep during most Hollywood movies. Still, what began in the barrios of south Los Angeles, California still informs my attention to detail: *Capri Suns* were really good in the California summer. Now, my wife reminds me of all the sugar that they have. I want my *Capri Sun.* I played the game. I gained. I lost.

To be continued, with love. Juan F. Carrillo

REFERENCES

Anyon, J. (1997). *Ghetto schooling: A political economy of urban educational reform*. New York, NY: Teachers College Press.

Anzaldúa, G. (1987). *Borderlands, La Frontera*. San Fracisco, CA: Aunt Lute Books.

Anzaldúa, G. (1990). Haciendo caras, una entrada. In G. Anzaldúa (Ed.), *Making face, making soul: Haciendo caras* (pp. xv–xxviii). San Francisco, CA: Aunt Lute Books.

Apple, M. (1978). The new sociology of education: Analyzing cultural and economic reproduction. *Harvard Educational Review, 48*, 495–503.

Asencio, M., & Acosta, K. (2010). Introduction: Mapping Latina/o sexualities research and scholarship. In M. Asencio (Ed.), *Latina/o sexualities: Probing powers, passions, practices, and policies* (pp. 1–12). Piscataway, NJ: Rutgers University Press.

Baca Zinn, M. (1982). Chicano men and masculinity. *Journal of Ethnic Studies, 10*(2), 29–44.

Baldwin, J. (1985). *The price of the ticket: Collected nonfiction 1948–1985*. New York, NY: St. Martin's Press.

Bartolomé, L. I. (1998). *The misteaching of academic discourses: The politics of language in the classroom*. Boulder, CO: Westview Press.

Beckett, S. (1982). *Waiting for Godot: A tragicomedy in two acts*. New York, NY: Grove Press.

Bernal, E. M. (1979). The education of the culturally different and gifted. In H. Passow (Ed.), *The gifted and talented: Their education and development—The seventy Fifth yearbook of the National Society for the Study of Education, Part I* (pp. 395–400). Chicago, IL: University of Chicago Press.

Bernal, E. M., Jr., & Reyna, J. (1974). *Analysis of giftedness in Mexican American children and design of a prototype identification instrument*. Washington, DC: Office of Education; Office for Gifted and Talented.

Berry, K. S. (2004). Multiple intelligences are not what they seem to be. In J. L. Kincheloe (Ed.), *Multiple intelligences reconsidered* (pp. 236–250). New York, NY: Peter Lang.

Bettie, J. (2003). *Women without class: Girls, race, and identity*. Berkeley, CA: University of California Press.

Bhabha, H. K. (1994). *The location of culture*. New York, NY: Routledge.

Bourdieu, P. (1984). *Distinction: A social critique of the judgment of taste*. Cambridge, MA: Harvard University Press.

Bowles, S., & Gintis, H. (1976). *Schooling in capitalist America: Educational reform and the contradictions of economic life*. New York, NY: Basic Books.

Briggs, C. J., & Reis, S. M. (2004). An introduction to the topic of cultural diversity and giftedness. In C. A. Tomlinson, D. Y. Ford, S. M. Reis, C. J. Briggs, & C. A. Strickland (Ed.), *In search of a dream: Designing classrooms that work for high potential students from diverse cultural background* (pp. 5–32). Washington, DC: National Association for Gifted Children.

Cammarota, J. (2008). *Suenos Americanos: Barrio youth negotiating social and cultural worlds*. Tucson, AZ: University of Arizona Press.

Cantú, N., & Fránquiz, M. (2010). *Inside the Latin@ experience: A Latin@ studies reader.* New York, NY: Palgrave Macmillan.

Carrillo, J. F. (2007). Lost in degree: A Chicano Ph.D. student's search for missing clothes. *Journal of Latinos and Education, 6*(4), 347–350.

REFERENCES

Carrillo, J. F. (2010). *So far from home: Portraits of Mexican origin scholarship boys* (Doctoral dissertation). University of Texas, Austin, TX. Retrieved from http://hdl.handle.net/2152/ETD-UT-2010-05-848

Carrillo, J. F. (2013). I always knew I was gifted: Latino males and the Mestiz@ Theory of Intelligences (MTI). *Berkeley Review of Education, 4*(1), 69–95.

Carrillo, J. F., & Rodriguez, E. (2016). She doesn't even act Mexican: Smartness trespassing in the new south. *Race Ethnicity and Education, 19*(6), 1–11.

Carter, P. (2005). *Keeping it real: School success beyond Black and White*. New York, NY: Oxford University Press.

Carter, T., & Segura, R. D. (1979). *Mexican Americans in school: A decade of change*. Princeton, NJ: College Board.

Chesser, J. (2012, August 15). Hispanics in NC: Big numbers in small towns. *UNC Charlotte Urban Institute*. Retrieved from http://ui.uncc.edu/story/hispanic-latino-population-north-carolina-cities-census

Conchas, G. Q. (2006). *The color of success: Race and high achieving urban youth*. New York, NY: Teacher's College Press.

Conchas, G. Q., & Vigil, J. D. (2012). *Street smart, school smart: Urban poverty and the education of adolescent boys*. New York, NY: Teachers College Press.

Connell, R. W. (1995). *Masculinities*. Berkeley, CA: University of California Press.

Cuádraz, G. H. (1993). *Meritocracy (un)challenged: The making of a chicano andprofessoriate andprofessoriate class* (Doctoral dissertation). University of California, Berkeley, CA.

Cuádraz, G. H. (1996). Experiences of multiple marginality: A case study of Chicana "scholarship women." In C. Turner, M. Garcia, A. Nora, & L. I. Rendón (Eds.), *Racial and ethnic diversity in higher education* (pp. 210–222). Needham Heights, MA: Simon & Schuster.

Cuádraz, G. H. (1999). Stories of access and 'luck': Chicana/os, higher education, and the politics of incorporation. *Latino Studies Journal, 10*(1), 110–123.

Cuádraz, G. H. (2006). Myths, interpretation and the "politics of exceptionality: Chicana/o narratives of achievement." *Oral History Review, 33*(1), 83–105.

Cuádraz, G. H., & Pierce, J. L. (1994). From scholarship girls to scholarship women: Surviving the contradictions of race and class in the academy. *Explorations in Ethnic Studies, 17*, 21–44.

Delgado Bernal, D. (2001). Using a Chicana feminist epistemology in educational research. *Harvard Educational Review, 68*(4), 555–582.

Delgado Bernal, D., Elenes, A., Godinez, F. E., & Villenas, S. (2006). *Chicana/Latina education in everyday life: Feminist perspectives on pedagogy and epistemology*. Albany, NY: State University of New York Press.

Deloria Jr., V. (1999). *Spirit and reason: The Vine Deloria, Jr. reader*. Golden, CO: Fulcrum Publishing.

Diaz, J. (2007). *The brief and wondrous of life of Oscar Wao*. New York, NY: Penguin.

Dubois, W. E. B. (1903/1996). The souls of Black folk. In E. J. Sundquist (Ed.), *W. E. B. Dubois reader* (pp. 97–240). New York, NY: Oxford University Press.

Elenes, A. (2011). *Transforming borders: Chicana/o popular culture and pedagogy*. Lanham, MD: Lexington Books.

Emerson, R. M., Fretz, R. I., & Shaw, L. L. (1995). *Writing ethnographic fieldnotes*. Chicago, IL: University of Chicago Press.

Erlandson, D., Harris, E. L., Skipper, B. L., & Allen, S. D. (1993). *Doing naturalistic inquiry: A guide to methods.* Newbury Park, CA: Sage Publications.

Farrell, W. (1974). *The liberated man: Beyond masculinity-freeing men and their relationships with women.* New York, NY: Random House.

Feagin, J. R., Vera, H., & Imani, N. (1996). *The agony of education: Black students at White colleges and universities.* New York, NY: Routledge.

Ferguson, A. A. (2001). *Bad boys: Public schools in the making of Black masculinity.* Ann Arbor, MI: University of Michigan Press.

Fitzgerald, F. S. (1993). *The Great Gatsby.* Ware, Hertfordshire: Wordsworth Classics.

Flores, B. (2005). The intellectual presence of the deficit view of Spanish-speaking children in the educational literature during the 20th century. In P. Pedraza & M. Rivera (Eds.), *Latino education: An agenda for community action research* (pp. 75–98). New York, NY: Routledge.

Flores, N., & Rosa, J. (2015). Undoing appropriateness: Raciolinguistic ideologies and language diversity in education. *Harvard Educational Review, 85*(2), 149–171.

Foley, D. E. (1990). *Learning capitalist culture deep in the heart of Tejas.* Philadelphia, PA: University of Pennsylvania Press.

Ford, D. Y., & Harris III, J. (1994). Promoting achievement among gifted Black students: The efficacy of new definitions and identification practices. *Urban Education, 29*(202), 202–229. doi:10.1177/0042085994029002006

Fordham, S., & Ogbu, J. U. (1986). Black students' school success: Coping with the burden of acting White. *The Urban Review, 18*(3), 176–206. doi:10.1007/BF01112192

Freire, P. (1970). *Pedagogy of the oppressed.* New York, NY: Continuum.

Freire, P. (1974). *Education for critical consciousness.* New York, NY: Continuum.

Freire, P., & Macedo, D. (1987). *Literacy: Reading the word and the world.* South Hadley, MA: Bergin & Garvey Publishers.

Gándara, P. (1995). *Over the ivory walls: The educational mobility of low income Chicanos.* Albany, NY: State University of New York.

García, O., & Leiva, C. (2014). Theorizing and enacting translanguaging for social justice. In A. Blackledge & A. Creese (Eds.), *Heteroglossia as practice and pedagogy* (pp. 199–216). Netherlands: Springer.

Gardner, H. (1985). *Frames of mind: The theory of multiple intelligences.* New York, NY: Basic Books.

Gardner, H. (1999). *Intelligence reframed: Multiple intelligences for the 21st Century.* New York, NY: Basic Books.

Gardner, H. (2006). *Multiple intelligences: New horizons.* New York, NY: Basic Books.

Gibson, M. (1988). *Accommodation without Assimilation: Sikh Immigrants in an American High School.* Ithaca, NY: Cornell University.

Gladwell, M. (2013). *David and Goliath: Underdogs, misfits, and the art of battling giants.* New York, NY: Hachette Book Group.

Gonzalez, G. G. (2014). Culture, language, and the Americanization of Mexican children. In A. Darder & R. Torres (Eds.), *Latinos and education: A critical reader* (pp. 158–173). New York, NY: Routledge.

Gramsci, A. (1971/2000). *Selections from the prison notebooks.* New York, NY: International Publishers.

Haraway, D. (1988). Situated knowledges: The science question in feminism as a site of discourse on the privilege of partial perspective. *Feminist Studies, 14*, 575–599. doi:10.2307/3178066

Harding, S. (1993). Rethinking standpoint epistemology: "What is strong objectivity?". In L. Alcoff & E. Potter (Eds.), *Feminist epistemologies* (pp. 49–82). New York, NY: Routledge.

Hatt, B. (2007). Street smarts vs. book smarts: The figured world of smartness in the lives of marginalized, urban youth. *The Urban Review, 39*(2), 145–166. doi:10.1007/s11256-007-0047-9

Hatt, B. (2011). Smartness as a cultural practice in schools. *American Educational Research Journal, 20*(10), 1–23. doi:10.3102/0002831211415661

Hoggart, R. (1957/2006). *The uses of literacy*. New Brunswick, NJ: Transaction Publishers.

Hokheimer, M., & Adorno, T. W. (2007). *The dialectic of enlightenment*. New York, NY: Continuum.

Kane, W. (2010, November 13). Latino kids now majority in state's public schools. *San Francisco Gate*. Retrieved from http://www.sfgate.com/education/article/Latino-kids-now-majority-in-state-s-public-schools-3166843.php

Kierkegaard, S. (2009). *Fear and trembling*. New York, NY: Feather Trail Press.

Kincheloe, J. L. (2004). Twenty-first-century questions about multiple intelligences. In J. L. Kincheloe (Ed.), *Multiple intelligences reconsidered* (pp. 3–28). New York, NY: Peter Lang.

Kincheloe, J. L., & Steinberg, S. R. (1997). Who said it can't happen here? In J. L. Kinchelo, S. R. Steinberg, & A. D. Gresson, III (Eds.), *Measured lies: The bell curve examined* (pp. 3–47). New York, NY: St. Martin's Press.

Kincheloe, J. L., Steinberg, S. R., & Tippins, D. J. (1999). *The stigma of genius: Einstein, consciousness, and education*. New York, NY: Peter Lang.

Kirkland, D. E. (2013). *A search past silence: The literacy of young Black men*. New York, NY: Teachers College Press.

Latina Feminist Group. (2001). *Telling to live: Latina feminist testimonios*. Durham, NC: Duke University Press.

Lawrence-Lightfoot, S., & Davis, J. H. (1997). *The art and science of portraiture*. San Francisco, CA: Jossey Bass.

Lopez, N. (2002). *Hopeful girls, troubled boys: Race and gender disparity in urban education*. New York, NY: Routledge.

Lopez, N. (2011). Racially stigmatized masculinities and empowerment: Conceptualizing and nurturing Latino males' schooling in the United States. In P. Noguera, A. Hurtado, & E. Fergus (Eds.), *Invisible no more: Understanding the disenfranchisement of Latino men and boys* (pp. 235–254). New York, NY: Routledge.

Maxwell, L. A. (2014, August 20). U.S. school enrollment hits majority-minority enrollment milestone. *Education Week*. Retrieved from http://www.edweek.org/ew/articles/2014/08/20/01demographics.h34.html

Mignolo, W. (2007). 'DELINKING': The rhetoric of modernity, the logic of coloniality and the grammar of de-coloniality. *Cultural Studies, 21*(2), 449–514. doi:10.1080/09502380601162647

Mirandé, A. (1997). *Hombres y Machos*. Boulder, CO: Westview Press.

Mohanty, C. T. (2003). *Feminism without borders: Decolonizing theory, practicing solidarity*. Durham, NC: Duke University Press.

Moll, L., Amanti, C., Neff, D., & Gonzalez, N. (1992). Funds of knowledge for teaching: Using a qualitative approach to connect homes and classrooms. *Theory Into Practice, 31*(2), 132–141. doi:10.1080/00405849209543534

Noguera, P., Hurtado, A., & Fergus, E. (Eds.). (2012). *Invisible no more: Understanding the disenfranchisement of Latino men and boys*. New York, NY: Routledge.

Ogbu, J. (1978). *Minority education and caste: The American system in cross-cultural perspective*. New York, NY: Academic Press.

Ogbu, J. (1987). Variability in minority school performance: A problem in search of an explanation. *Anthropology in Education Quarterly, 18*(4), 312–334.

Paz, O. (1985). *The labyrinth of solitude*. New York, NY: Grove Press.

Pérez II, D. (2014). Exploring the nexus between community cultural wealth and the academic and social experiences of Latino male achievers. *International Journal of Qualitative Studies in Education, 27*(6), 747–767

Pérez-Torres, R. (2006). *Mestizaje: Critical uses of race in Chicano culture*. Minneapolis, MN: University of Minnesota Press.

Pizarro, M. (2005). *Chicanas and Chicanos in schools: Racial profiling, identity battles, and empowerment*. Austin, TX: University of Texas Press.

Poole, R. (2008). Memory, history and the claims of the past. *Memory Studies, 1*(2), 149–166.

Rendón, L. (1992). From the Barrio to the academy: Revelations of a Mexican American "Scholarship Girl." In *New directions for community colleges* (Vol. 80, pp. 55–64). San Francisco, CA: Jossey-Bass.

Ríos Vega, J. A. (2015). *Counterstorytelling narratives of Latino teenage boys: From Verguenza to ́Echale Ganas*. NewYork, NY: Peter Lang.

Rios, V. M. (2011). *Punished: Policing the lives of Black and Latino boys*. New York, NY: New York University Press.

Rodríguez, J. M. (2003). *Queer Latinidad: Identity practices, discursive spaces*. New York, NY: New York University Press.

Rodriguez, R. (1975). Going home again: The new American scholarship boy. *American Scholar, 44*(1), 15–28.

Rodriguez, R. (1982). *Hunger of memory: The education of Richard Rodriguez*. New York, NY: Random House.

Rodriguez, R. (1992). *Days of obligation: An argument with my Mexican father*. New York, NY: Penguin Books.

Rodriguez, R. (2002). *Brown: The last discovery of America*. London, England: Penguin Books.

Rodriguez, R. (2013). *Darling: A spiritual autobiography*. New York, NY: Penguin Books.

Rose, M. (1989). *Lives on the boundary: A moving account of the struggles and achievements of America's educationally underprepared*. New York, NY: Penguin Group.

Saenz, V. B., & Ponjuan, L. (2009). The vanishing Latino male in higher education. *Journal of Hispanic Higher Education, 8*(1), 54–89. doi:10.1177/1538192708326995

Sáenz, V. B., & Ponjuan, L. (2011). *Men of color: Ensuring the academic success of Latino males in higher education*. Retrieved from http://www.ihep.org/sites/default/files/uploads/docs/pubs/brief_men_of_color_latinos.pdf

Sáenz, V. B., Ponjuan, L., & Figueroa, J. (Eds.). (2016). *Ensuring the success of Latino males in higher education: A new national imperative*. Sterling, VA: Stylus Publishing, LLC.

Sandoval, C. (2000). *Methodology of the oppressed*. Minneapolis, MN: University of Minnesota Press.

Sennet, R., & Cobb, J. (1972). *The hidden injuries of class*. New York, NY: Norton.

Staiger, A. (2004). Whiteness as giftedness: Racial formation at an urban high school. *Social Problems, 51*(2), 161–181.

Stanton Salazar, R. D. (2001). *Manufacturing hope and despair*. New York, NY: Teachers College Press.

Suzuki, L. A., & Valencia, R. (1997). Race-ethnicity and measured intelligence: Educational implications. *American Psychologist, 52*(10), 1103–1114. doi:10.1037/0003-066X.52.10.1103

Thoreau, H. D. (2004). *Walden; or, life in the woods* (J. Cramer, Ed.). New Haven, CT: Yale University Press.

Torres, M., & Fergus, E. (2011). Social mobility and the complex status of Latino males: Education, employment, and incarceration patterns 2000–2009. In P. Noguera, A. Hurtado, & E. Fergus (Eds.), *Invisible no more: Understanding the disenfranchisement of Latino men and boys* (pp. 19–40). New York, NY: Routledge. (published 1854)

Trueba, H. T. (1988). Culturally based explanations of minority students academic achievement. *Anthropology and Education Quarterly, 19*(4), 270–285.

Urrieta, L., Jr. (2009). *Working from within: Chicana and Chicano activist educators in whitestream schools*. Tucson, AZ: University of Arizona Press.

Valdés, G. (2003). *Expanding definitions of giftedness: The case of young interpreters from immigrant families*. Mahwah, NJ: Lawrence Erlbaum.

Valencia, R. R. (2002). The explosive growth of the Chicano/Latino population: Educational Implications. In R. R. Valencia (Ed.), *Chicano school failure and success: Past, present, and future* (pp. 52–59). New York, NY: Routledge.

Valencia, R. R., Villarreal, B. J., & Salinas, M. F. (2002). Educational testing and Chicano students: Issues, consequences, and prospects for reform. In R. R. Valencia (Ed.), *Chicano school failure and success: Past, present, and future* (2nd ed., pp. 253–309). New York, NY: Routledge Falmer.

Valenzuela, A. (1999). *Subtractive schooling: U.S. Mexican youth and the politics of caring*. Albany, NY: State University of New York.

Villenas, S. (2001). Latina mothers and small-town racisms: Creating narratives of dignity and moral education in North Carolina. *Anthropology and Education Quarterly, 32*(1), 3–28.

Weiss, R. S. (1994). *Learning from strangers: The art and method of qualitative interview studies*. New York, NY: The Free Press.

Willis, P. (1977). *Learning to labor*. Aldershot, UK: Gower.

Yosso, T. (2006). Whose cultural capital? A critical race theory discussion of community cultural wealth. *Race, Ethnicity, and Education, 8*(1), 69–91.

Zavella, P. (1991). Reflecting on diversity among Chicanas. *Frontiers: A Journal of Women's Studies, 12*(2), 73–85. doi:10.2307/3346849

CPSIA information can be obtained
at www.ICGtesting.com
Printed in the USA
BVHW01s2305270118
506496BV00002B/40/P

9 789463 007658